D0700015

UNDERSTANDING
CARSON McCULLERS

Understanding Contemporary American Literature

Matthew J. Bruccoli, *Editor*

Understanding Bernard Malamud
by Jeffrey Helterman
Understanding James Dickey
by Ronald Baughman
Understanding John Hawkes
by Donald J. Greiner
Understanding Thomas Pynchon
by Robert D. Newman
Understanding Randall Jarrell
by J. A. Bryant, Jr.
Understanding Edward Albee
by Matthew C. Roudané
Understanding Contemporary American Drama
by William Herman
Understanding Vladimir Nabokov
by Stephen Jan Parker
Understanding Joyce Carol Oates
by Greg Johnson
Understanding Theodore Roethke
by Walter B. Kalaidjian
Understanding Mary Lee Settle
by George Garrett
Understanding Isaac Bashevis Singer
by Lawrence S. Friedman
Understanding George Garrett
by R. H. W. Dillard
Understanding Walker Percy
by Linda Whitney Hobson
Understanding Chicano Literature
by Carl R. Shirley and Paula W. Shirley
Understanding Denise Levertov
by Harry Marten
Understanding Raymond Carver
by Arthur M. Saltzman
Understanding Katherine Anne Porter
by Darlene Harbour Unrue
Understanding Robert Bly
by William V. Davis
Understanding William Stafford
by Judith Kitchen

UNDERSTANDING Carson McCULLERS

by VIRGINIA SPENCER CARR

UNIVERSITY OF SOUTH CAROLINA PRESS

First Edition

Published in Columbia, South Carolina, by the
University of South Carolina Press

Manufactured in the United States of America

Library of Congress Cataloging-in-Publication Data

Carr, Virginia Spencer.
Understanding Carson McCullers / by Virginia Spencer Carr.
p. cm. — (Understanding contemporary American literature)
Includes bibliographical references.
ISBN 0-87249-661-9
1. McCullers, Carson, 1917–1967 — Criticism and interpretation.
I. Title. II. Series.
PS3525.A1772Z582 1989
813'.52—dc20 89-22672
CIP

For

Michael McClard Gale

and

Sarah Spencer Gale

CONTENTS

EDITOR'S PREFACE

Understanding Contemporary American Literature has been planned as a series of guides or companions for students as well as good nonacademic readers. The editor and publisher perceive a need for these volumes because much of the influential contemporary literature makes special demands. Uninitiated readers encounter difficulty in approaching works that depart from the traditional forms and techniques of prose and poetry. Literature relies on conventions, but the conventions keep evolving; new writers form their own conventions—which in time may become familiar. Put simply, *UCAL* provides instruction in how to read certain contemporary writers—identifying and explicating their material, themes, use of language, point of view, structures, symbolism, and responses to experience.

The word *understanding* in the series title was deliberately chosen. Many willing readers lack an adequate understanding of how contemporary literature works; that is, what the author is attempting to express and the means by which it is conveyed. Although the criticism and analysis in the series have been aimed at a level of general accessibility, these introductory volumes are meant to be applied in conjunction with the works they cover. Thus they do not provide a substitute for the works and authors they introduce, but rather prepare the reader for more profitable literary experiences.

M. J. B.

ACKNOWLEDGMENTS

Grateful acknowledgment is made to Houghton Mifflin Company for permission to quote from the copyrighted works of Carson McCullers and from "Some Words Before," my introduction to *Collected Stories of Carson McCullers: Including "The Member of the Wedding" and "The Ballad of the Sad Café"* (1987); to Oxmoor House, Inc., Birmingham, Alabama, for permission to quote from my essay, "Carson McCullers and *The Heart Is a Lonely Hunter:* A Commentary" (1984); to Gale Research Company, Detroit, for permission to quote from my essay, "Carson McCullers," in *Contemporary Authors: Bibliographical Series, American Novelists,* ed. James J. Martine (1986); to *The Southern Quarterly Review* for permission to quote from my essay, "Carson McCullers, Novelist Turned Playwright" (1987).

Had I not already been deeply immersed in the life and work of this Georgia-born author for over two decades, *Understanding Carson McCullers* might have been a more conventional book in the *Understanding Contemporary American Literature Series.* As McCullers's biographer I have been too long accustomed to looking at her life as a means of illuminating her fiction to take a more traditional approach as a literary critic. Yet I think I have succeeded in examining her work and tracing her artistic vision within the prescribed parameters of this series, the providing of "instruction in how to read certain contemporary writers." Thus, to "understand" McCullers's work, to appreciate more fully her themes, use of language, point of view, and other characteristics of her fiction is to be privy, also, to her creative process: an intricate layering of experience and imagination, a fictional response to experience that she thought of, paradoxically, as a "Divine collusion."

I thank, especially, Roger Harris for his suggestions, editorial assistance, and generous sharing through every phase of the manuscript. I am also grateful to Caroline Blumenthal for her meticulous research assistance; to Patricia Bryan, Sonja Gardner, Laurie Scott, and Anita Williams for their assistance in the preparation of the final manuscript; to Kristan Sarvé-Gorham for her indexing and reading of galley proofs; to Mary Robbins for her careful reading of the manuscript; to Matthew C. Roudané for his advice as a seasoned author in this series; to Clyde W. Faulkner, Dean of the College of Arts and Sciences of Georgia State University, for his support of my project; and to Aimee Alexander, Professor of English Emeritus at Eastern Kentucky University, with whom I have discussed McCullers's writings for over a decade and, in the process, gleaned new insights into the art and mind of the author.

I gratefully acknowledge, too, the permission of Louise Dahl-Wolfe for the use of her photograph of Carson McCullers on the cover of this book.

Finally, I appreciate the help of Kenneth J. Scott, Director of the University of South Carolina Press, and his staff in helping see this manuscript through production.

UNDERSTANDING
CARSON McCULLERS

CHAPTER ONE

Understanding Carson McCullers

Life and Overview of Career

Carson McCullers left behind an impressive literary legacy when she died at the age of fifty in 1967: four novels, a novella, two plays, twenty short stories, some two dozen nonfiction pieces (published in such magazines as *Vogue, Harper's Bazaar, Mademoiselle, The New Yorker, Redbook, McCall's, Esquire,* and *Saturday Review*), a book of children's verse, and a handful of poems. McCullers was beset by ill health for over half of her life (having suffered three crippling strokes before she was thirty), yet she managed to write almost daily.

She began her extraordinary career at twenty-three upon publication of her first novel, *The Heart Is a Lonely Hunter* (1940). The book is set in a small southern mill town resembling Columbus, Georgia, where she was born Lula Carson Smith—the oldest of three children—on February 19, 1917. The novel reflects vividly the author's milieu in the 1930s and is her most autobiographical tale.

A finely chiseled second novel, *Reflections in a Golden Eye* (1941), was called a chilling tour de force, a bizarre tale set on an army post not unlike Fort Benning, Georgia, which McCullers knew well, having taken piano lessons there from the wife of its infantry school commander. Critics alternately praised and damned the novel, while readers in general objected to the morbid behavior of its characters.

The author herself was partial to her novella, *The Ballad of the Sad Café* (1943), which appeared originally in *Harper's Bazaar* and later as the title story of an omnibus edition, *"The Ballad of the Sad Café": The Novels and Stories of Carson McCullers* (1951). The novella and her third novel, *The Member of the Wedding* (1946), are generally considered her finest work. McCullers reached a new audience with her theatrical adaptation of *The Member of the Wedding,* which won most of the theater awards in 1950 and ran for 501 performances on Broadway. The play solidified her popular success, but had little bearing upon her critical reputation. In 1957 a second play, *The Square Root of Wonderful,* opened on Broadway and closed in seven weeks, opening night reviewers having declared it a disaster.

McCullers's readers who knew of her increasingly debilitating illnesses waited apprehensively for *Clock Without Hands* (1961), her final novel, which climbed to sixth place on the *New York Times* bestseller list amidst mixed reviews. Three years later, *Sweet as a Pickle and Clean as a Pig* (1964), a collection of verse for children, was released, her last book before her death in 1967. *The Mortgaged Heart* (1971), a posthumous volume of short pieces edited by Margarita Gachet Smith, McCullers's sister, is notable for its outline of "The Mute" (*The Heart is a Lonely Hunter*), but critics saw little merit in her previously unpublished apprentice tales. They welcomed, however, the availability under one cover of her nonfiction pieces and many of her best short stories. In 1987 all of McCullers's short fiction, save one slight piece ("The March"), was published in *Collected Stories of Carson McCullers Including: "The Member of the Wedding" and "The Ballad of the Sad Café,"* with an introduction by Virginia Spencer Carr.

Critics continue to compare and contrast McCullers with Eudora Welty, Flannery O'Connor, and Katherine Anne Porter, whom they generally consider to be better stylists in the short form than McCullers. Yet they tend to rank McCullers above her female contemporaries as a novelist. McCullers herself had a keen appreciation of her own work without regard to the sex of those with whom she was compared. "Surely I have more to say than Hemingway, and God knows, I say it better than Faulkner," she once boasted.[1] Some scholars link her to Thomas Wolfe, Sherwood Anderson, and William Saroyan and liken her cold, pure style, her impersonal point of view, and her use of symbolism to that written in the Flaubertian tradition. McCullers herself commented that she wrote in the tradition of the Russian realists and attributed this inclination to her southern heritage.[2] Others readily see elements of Hawthorne and Poe in her tendency toward the grotesque in her novels. In her poetic sensibility she reminds readers of Graham Greene, D. H. Lawrence, and Faulkner. Whatever the linkage, influences, tags, and scholarly attention that McCullers's work regularly receives, her novels, short stories, and plays continue to be read and written about appreciatively by American and foreign critics alike. Her fiction has been translated into over thirty languages, and academic studies of it abound, especially, in France, England, Canada, and Japan.

McCullers was descended on both sides from solid middle-class families in the Deep South for whom tradition and a sense of place were more important than wealth and material possessions. Her father (Lamar Smith) was a jeweler and watch repairman, and her mother (Marguerite Waters Smith) had worked for a time for the jeweler who employed him before he had his own store. The Smiths were regarded by their friends and neighbors—and by the townsfolk in general—as a highly respectable family of moderate means. While growing up in Georgia, McCullers was called by her double name, Lula Carson, in the southern manner, having been named for her maternal grandmother, Lula Carson Waters. Her great-grandfather was Major John Carson, whose seventy-five slaves and two thousand acres of rich farmland on Georgia's Flint River provoked envy and admiration throughout the region (until Wilson's Raiders set fire to his cotton stores and freed his slaves). The major never returned to his devastated lands and family, for he died on a Civil War battlefield in Virginia. As a child McCullers relished the tales of her hapless kinsmen who died in the war and the strong-willed women who survived them, but she was also vaguely disquieted by the paradoxes and inequalities of life in the South and rejected early the stereotypical standards imposed upon women of her generation. At thirteen she insisted on being called *Carson* and refused to answer again to her double name.

McCullers surmised at an early age that she was no ordinary child, her mother having informed her—or so the story went—that certain "prenatal signs" presaged that her firstborn would be a genius, a flowering awaited by Marguerite Smith with an air of buoyant expectancy. At age six McCullers confirmed the prophecy (in her mother's eyes, at least), by sitting down at the piano and playing with both hands a song she had heard for the first time that afternoon in a movie theater. At ten she began her formal training in piano. To become a concert pianist was her driving passion by the time she was thirteen and studying with a new teacher, Mary Tucker, whom she worshiped. McCullers was seventeen when her intensive study was interrupted by what doctors called "pneumonia with complications" (later diagnosed as rheumatic fever), whereupon the young pianist not only began to question her stamina for a concert career, but also to concede that her cleverness at the keyboard may have been more a reflection of her rigorous regime of daily practice than of musical genius. Too weak to play the piano during her long recuperation, McCullers began to write brooding, macabre dramas in imitation of Eugene O'Neill, and soon she was casting, directing, and producing plays at home before an audience of relatives and neighbors.

An ordinary student in high school, McCullers had no interest in a traditional college education. Instead, she asked her cousin, a librarian, to make up a list for her of "the greatest literature in the world" and insisted that she would "read it all."[3] To read was to prepare to be a writer, and where better to read and learn to write than in New York City, she reasoned. Unheard of as it was in Columbus, Georgia, in the early 1930s for a young woman to traipse off alone to New York City, McCullers convinced her mother that she wanted to prepare for a concert career at the Juilliard School of Music. She had already informed her piano teacher, however, that she was giving up music to become a writer, having felt abandoned when Mary Tucker told her that her husband was being transferred from Fort Benning to a distant city out of state, and that her young pupil would have to study with someone else.

McCullers was barely seventeen when she arrived in Manhattan, where she coped not only with being on her own for the first time in an alien city, but also with an often hostile environment in the grips of the Great Depression. She ate sparingly, lived in a succession of residence "clubs" for young women, and took odd jobs to support herself and to pay her tuition. She boasted later that she never voluntarily left a position but was fired regularly for daydreaming or reading Proust on her employer's time. She made no effort to enroll at Juilliard, but studied, instead, for two years at Columbia University with some of the best creative writing teachers in the city: Whit Burnett, Dorothy Scarborough, and Helen Rose Hull. She also took classes with Sylvia Chatfield Bates, who was considered New York University's most successful teacher of creative writing. McCullers soon shifted her interest from playwriting to fiction, and her teachers during her second year in the city—Burnett and Bates—quickly recognized her extraordinary promise.

Repeated attacks of pernicious anemia, pleurisy, and other respiratory ailments related to her still undiagnosed rheumatic fever interrupted McCullers's formal studies and frequently drove her south to recuperate. In 1935, during one such visit home, she met Reeves McCullers, a Fort Benning soldier from Wetumpka, Alabama, who was also an aspiring writer. On September 20, 1937, they were married in the Smith family home in Columbus and moved to Charlotte, North Carolina, where Reeves—now a civilian—found work as a credit investigator.

McCullers said that she was still on her honeymoon when she began work on the elusive tale that she had worried over for months, a manuscript entitled "The Mute." In less than a year she had a detailed outline and six chapters ready to submit to a fiction-writing contest sponsored by Houghton Mifflin, which won for her a special prize of $500 (an advance against royalties) and a promise of publication if the work proved satisfactory. She finished her novel in 1939 while living in Fayetteville, North Carolina, a small army town to which her husband had been transferred.

On June 4, 1940, McCullers was in Manhattan for the release of "The Mute," now retitled *The Heart Is a Lonely Hunter.* To her utter amazement and delight, she discovered that editors and critics alike considered her the "publisher's 'find' of the decade."[4] But by this time her early romantic notion of a fruitful married life with Reeves McCullers had soured, and she found herself caught up in a literary and artistic circle that included W. H. Auden, George Davis, Gypsy Rose Lee, Richard Wright, Peter Pears, Benjamin Britten, Chester Kallman, Oliver Smith, and Paul Bowles—all of whom lived together intermittently in a loose boardinghouse arrangement (presided over by Auden) in a quaint old brownstone at 7 Middagh Street in Brooklyn Heights, New York. Visitors dubbed the building "February House" or "The House of Pisces" when they became aware that many of its colorful residents were born in

February. McCullers lived in the household from time to time (without Reeves) for four years, during which she became an intimate, also, of Janet Flanner, David Diamond, Muriel Rukeyser, Klaus Mann, Granville Hicks, Louis Untermeyer, Newton Arvin, Truman Capote, and later, of Isak Dinesen, Edith Sitwell, Elizabeth Bowen, and Tennessee Williams. "Carson was enough to drive any small town right off its rocker and stood out among New Yorkers, even, as an eccentric of the first water," declared Flanner ("Genet" of *The New Yorker*).[5] Eleanor Clark, who noted that "Carson loved to shock and say outlandish things," recalled McCullers's telling her: "I must go home periodically to renew my sense of horror."[6]

Soon after her move north, McCullers became enamored of a Swiss novelist, Annemarie Clarac-Schwarzenbach, who was living temporarily in Manhattan, and her husband fell in love with their best friend, David Diamond, whom he lived with for five months in Rochester, New York. McCullers was more upset by Reeves's having deprived her of their best friend, her "we of me"—a concept that turned up regularly in her fiction later—than she was by his having "abandoned her" for a man. Equally devastating was her discovery that Reeves had absconded with some of her royalty checks. She sued for divorce on the only admissible grounds in New York in 1941: adultery.

In the 1940s McCullers was invited often to Yaddo Artists Colony in Saratoga Springs, New York, where she was attracted, in turn, to a succession of women. Charismatic, fey, admittedly androgynous, and considered a lesbian by her friends in New York (a side of her quite unknown to her family and friends in Georgia), she craved love and companionship and developed outrageous crushes on women she barely knew.[7] She occasionally fell in love with men as well, but such attachments were largely platonic.

In 1943 Reeves McCullers rejoined the Army as a newly commissioned second lieutenant and was ordered to the European front as a company commander in the U.S. Army Rangers. Before leaving, he wrote his wife a conciliatory letter in which he vowed that he still loved her and had put his "foolish ways" behind him.[8] Despite her bitter memories of their worst days, McCullers went to see Reeves, and throughout the war they wrote devotedly to one another. In 1945 they remarried, Reeves having returned from the war a decorated and injured hero. The marriage proved a mistake from the outset. Reeves resented his wife's increasing invalidism and petulant demands upon him, and she was progressively aggrieved by his uncontrolled alcoholism and violent, unpredictable actions. He committed suicide in Paris on November 19, 1953. Yet despite her two troubled marriages and her many debilitating illnesses, McCullers managed to keep on writing almost daily. Whereas the friends and acquaintances upon whom she relied for her emotional and physical nurturing sometimes disappointed her, she could always count on the characters in her fiction to behave as she predicted, even in their debasement. When Edith Sitwell wrote McCullers from London to express her great admiration for her fiction, the author replied that writing was her "search for God."[9] She told a longtime friend in her hometown during her last trip to the Deep South, "I wouldn't want to live if I couldn't write,"[10] and to a reporter in 1963, she said simply: "Writing is not only how I earn my living; it is how I earn my soul."[11]

McCullers was nearly devastated when her widowed mother—with whom she shared a home in Nyack, New York—died in 1955, and for the next twelve years, she lived alone, increasingly frail, in the old Victorian frame house that overlooked the Hudson River. Friends and admirers stopped in from time to time to visit, a longtime housekeeper continued to meet her immediate needs, and a cousin who lived in New York City (Jordan Massee) was devoted to her. She depended most, however, upon Dr. Mary Mercer, a psychiatrist who supervised her medical treatment and was her closest companion for a decade.

McCullers suffered a massive brain hemorrhage and lay comatose for forty-seven days until her death on September 29, 1967, at age fifty. She was buried beside her mother in Oak Hill Cemetery in Nyack, their graves marked by identical stones of Georgia marble.

Notes

1. Robert Ryan to Virginia Spencer Carr, letter, 8 Oct. 1970.

2. Carson McCullers, "The Russian Realists and Southern Literature," *The Mortgaged Heart*, ed. Margarita G. Smith (Boston: Houghton Mifflin, 1971), 252–258.

3. Virginia Johnson Storey to Carr, interview, Columbus, Ga., 19 May 1970; see also Carr, *The Lonely Hunter: A Biography of Carson McCullers* (Garden City: Doubleday, 1975), 32–33.

4. Kenneth McCormick to Carr, interview, New York City, 5 Sept. 1971.

5. Janet Flanner to Carr, interview, New York City, 1 Mar. 1972.

6. Eleanor Clark to Carr, letter, 15 Oct. 1973.

7. M. Segrest, "Lines I Dare to Write: Lesbian Writing in the South," *Southern Exposure* 9 [2] (1981): 53–62. In her discussion of the work of various southern lesbian writers of fiction, Segrest analyzes McCullers's themes and concerns. She claims that McCullers acted out of "lesbian alienation" and states that "it is no wonder that loneliness and displacement suffuse her writing and are seen as cosmic."

8. Carson McCullers to David Diamond, undated letter [Oct. 1943], from private collection, David Diamond, Rochester, N.Y.

9. Carson McCullers to Dame Edith Sitwell, letter, 8 Sept. 1959, Edith Sitwell Collection, New York City Public Library.

10. Mrs. George Swift, Jr., to Carr, interview, Columbus, Ga., 29 Sept. 1970.

11. "An Interview with Carson McCullers," *The Marquis* (Lafayette College) (1964): 22.

CHAPTER TWO

The Heart Is a Lonely Hunter

Carson McCullers worked on the manuscript that eventually became *The Heart Is a Lonely Hunter* under the influence of Sylvia Chatfield Bates, her creative writing teacher at New York University who had recommended her to Whit Burnett's short-story writing course at Columbia University. Believing in the young student's potential, Bates encouraged McCullers to submit a short story she had written in her class, "Wunderkind," to *Story* magazine, edited by Burnett. He bought the tale for publication in the December 1936 issue of *Story* and listened, also, to the long rambling plot of a novel that his young pupil explained had been gestating for almost a year.[1]

Several months later, while home in Georgia to recuperate from a rheumatic fever attack, McCullers wrote Burnett that she was working hard on her novel every day, but that it made no sense because her protagonist kept changing. She envisioned him first as John Minovich, a man in a small southern town to whom various people kept talking and relating their troubles; then she made him a Jew and called him Harry Minowitz, but the new characterization had no significant effect on the story line either. At last, suddenly and inexplicably as she paced a hooked rug in her living room—stepping on some designs and purposefully avoiding others—a wholly new protagonist emerged. "His name is John Singer, and he is a deaf mute," she exclaimed to her mother in the next room. When Marguerite Smith asked skeptically about the number of deaf mutes her daughter had known in her life, McCullers replied, "I've never known one, but I know Mr. Singer."[2] A few weeks later when her husband read that a "deaf and dumb convention" was being held in nearby Macon, Georgia, and suggested that they attend so that she could "see what a real deaf mute is like," McCullers was horrified by the mere suggestion. "Oh, no, there is nothing those people could tell me. I have already written that part of the novel," she insisted.[3] McCullers would not risk having her imagined image of John Singer jarred by confrontation with reality.

A comparison of the novel with McCullers's outline and synopsis submitted to Houghton Mifflin in 1938 confirms that her major characters and everything significant to the story line remained as she originally conceived them.[4] McCullers made it clear in the general remarks prefacing her outline that the story focused upon "five isolated, lonely people in their search for expression and spiritual integration with something greater than themselves."[5] She told editor Ralph McGill of the *Atlanta Journal-Constitution* that the novel's theme and characters unmistakably reflected her view of the conscience of the South: "The human heart is a lonely hunter—but the search for us Southerners is more anguished. There is a special guilt in us . . . a consciousness of guilt not fully knowable or communicable. Southerners are the more lonely and spiritually estranged, I think, because we have lived so long in an artificial social system that we insisted was natural and right and just—when all along we knew that it wasn't."[6]

John Singer, the deaf mute and pivotal character of *The Heart Is a Lonely Hunter,* is an apt vehicle for the author's perception of the abject loneliness and solitude inherent in the human condition. More important to the novel's plot and development of theme than Singer, however, are the other major characters: Mick Kelly, a tomboyish adolescent who shuts out the real world with music and dreams of fame and distant lands; Biff Brannon, the quietly observant and sexually impotent proprietor of the New York Café; Jake Blount, a fanatical carnival worker who seeks to redress the ills of the townspeople; and Dr. Benedict Mady Copeland, a proud, black physician whose people reject his Marxist ideals and fail to understand his ineffectual attempts to improve their lot. Each character is isolated from meaningful social discourse, and each sees his salvation in the mute. When Singer's world topples upon the death of his retarded companion, Spiros Antonapoulos (who is also a deaf mute), so, too, does theirs.

Had McCullers not had a strong background in musical theory, *The Heart Is a Lonely Hunter* doubtless would have been a very different work. She viewed the novel's intricate, three-part structure as a fugue, explaining that part 1 announces the broad theme of "man's revolt against his own inner isolation and his urge to express himself as fully as possible" as one voice, first through Singer, then through the other major characters, whose unique voices are introduced and developed contrapuntally in balanced order.[7] Each character takes on new texture and color as his presence and actions become interwoven with the others. McCullers adapted her writing style to approximate the different "inner psychic rhythms" of each character who commands his own chapter or whose point of view is being presented.[8]

Part 1, which opens with Singer, also closes with him. The four intervening chapters introduce the troubled lives of the other principal characters. Singer's dilemma is presented in a straightforward narrative marked by clean, sparse prose, and his two sections are almost pure exposition. Although the point of view appears to be rendered objectively through an omniscient narrator who is not a part of the tale itself, McCullers managed to convey a sympathetic portrayal of each character. The syntax and rhythms are marked by an Old Testament cadence, an absence of contractions, and many short, one-sentence paragraphs that announce and summarize, such as "And then the final trouble came to Singer" and "In the spring a change came over Singer." The style is reminiscent of a parable and, despite its austerity of language, is hauntingly lyrical. Like Singer himself, the tone of chapter 1 is quiet and muted, the action understated. "But still he wandered through the streets of the town, always silent and alone,"[9] the opening chapter concludes.

Part 2, which constitutes more than half the book, utilizes contrapuntal techniques as McCullers developed the anguished searches of Singer's satellites (the author's term for the characters who revolve around the mute) for some inexplicable connection, for love, compassion, and fulfillment of purpose. This section demonstrates that the inevitable failure of each person is brought on by a combination of free will and environmental entrapment. Fifteen chapters comprise part 2: five are devoted to Mick Kelly, two to Biff Brannon, four to Dr. Copeland, two to Jake Blount, and two to John Singer.[10] The characters interweave throughout this section, which concludes with Singer's death and defines what McCullers called the "main web of the story."[11]

Part 3 functions as a formal coda to the composition. In it the satellite characters, who have been set into orbit when their savior figure (Singer) commits suicide, return momentarily to voice their lamentations in mini-codas of their own (labeled *morning, afternoon, evening,* and *night*) that bring the fugue to a close. Their aggrieved situations—as well as the plight of the townspeople as a whole—are ultimately far worse than they were when Singer inadvertently entered their lives.

In an article entitled "*The Heart Is a Lonely Hunter*: A Literary Symphony," Barbara Farrelly argues convincingly that it was, in fact, *Eroica,* Beethoven's Third Symphony, which inspired McCullers to write such a novel. "[McCullers] heard what Beethoven heard. She heard 'the whole world'; she heard a novel, and then set it to literature."[12]

Although the broad setting is an unnamed, stagnant mill town in the Deep South in the late 1930s, most of the action in which the major characters come together contrapuntally occurs in Biff Brannon's New York Café or in John Singer's room. Their paths crisscross throughout the town—and each goes off his separate way for a time—but all are drawn repeatedly back to Singer, from whom they derive their spiritual and emotional enrichment, just as they are drawn again and again to the all-night diner for their physical nourishment. Ultimately, their spiritual and material needs—and the nurturing that ensues temporarily—become so enmeshed that the characters have little identity apart from each other.

The novel opens on the passive Singer, who is a silverware engraver, and Antonapoulos, his Greek companion with whom he has lived for ten years. The narrator informs the reader that they have no other friends and that nothing intrudes upon their routine of eating alone in their sparsely furnished two-room dwelling in the upstairs of a small house, going weekly to the library so that Singer could check out a mystery book, attending a Friday night movie, and having Antonapoulos's picture taken every payday in a ten-cent photograph shop. However, when Antonapoulos begins stealing ridiculous objects that he does not need and his habits become obscene, he is committed to the state asylum by his cousin, in whose fruit store he works. Alone and utterly desolate, Singer thinks only of his friend. Finally, the rooms themselves that they have shared become intolerable, and Singer moves to the Kelly family's makeshift boardinghouse near the center of town and begins taking his meals at the New York Café. It is at this point that the lonely mute becomes the pivotal character of the novel and the action rises.

Mick Kelly, Jake Blount, and Benedict Mady Copeland see in the thin soberly dressed mute a certain "mystic superiority" and ascribe to him in a kind of mirror counterpoint the qualities that they would like for him to have. He becomes, in effect, a repository of their own illusions and stored-up anguish. Although Singer appears to take an interest in his interlocutors, his inner life is inviolate. The others have no way of knowing that the mute's emotional life is rooted firmly in his feelings for his obese friend, Antonapoulos, or that Antonapoulos even exists. Moreover, the Greek is as incapable of perceiving Singer's love for him as Singer himself is in perceiving the admiration of those drawn to him.

Biff Brannon, McCullers's point-of-view character—who proves to be one of the most sympathetically drawn characters in McCullers's canon—has sat day and night for twenty-one years behind the cash register in his café, quietly observing his unhappy and frustrated customers and analyzing everything he sees. Despite his bizarre behavior, Brannon is probably the most balanced of all the characters in the novel. In her abstract of the book, McCullers wrote of the café proprietor's extravagant need to ingest details and of his "faculty for seeing the things which happen around him with cold objectivity—without instinctively connecting them with himself."[13] Consequently, Brannon's appearances in the novel are marked by a combination of simple exposition, straightforward narration, cryptic dialogue, and an objective reporting of his observations and habits, recollections, and interpretations. At times the storytelling method almost slips into a quasi-stream-of-consciousness technique with little distance between the omniscient narrator and Brannon himself. The reader becomes aware, also, of the theatricality of scenes in which this character appears, even though most of the action concerning Brannon is internal.[14]

A significant aspect of Brannon's social and moral separation is his alienation from Alice, his carping wife with whom he lives in a room above the café. Brannon is fascinated by freaks (much to Alice's dismay), and the more deformed they are, the more generous he is with the liquor in his café: "Whenever somebody with a harelip or T.B. came into the place he would set him up to beer. Or if the customer were a hunchback or a bad cripple, then it would be whiskey on the house. There was one fellow who had had his peter and his left leg blown off in a boiler explosion, and whenever he came to town there was a free pint waiting for him" (17–18).

Throughout the tale Brannon is attracted to the gangly, androgynous Mick Kelly, who, more than any of the other characters, most engages the reader. Brannon mistakes Mick for a boy when she comes into the café after midnight to buy cigarettes. She is thirteen at the opening of the tale, and she smokes to stunt her growth.[15] Brannon thinks uneasily of Mick's "hoarse, boyish voice and of her habit of hitching up her khaki shorts and swaggering like a cowboy in the picture show" (17). The next year, when she is a student at Vocational High and her daily garb is a red sweater and blue pleated skirt, he observes that she still "looked as much like an overgrown boy as a girl" and asks himself why "was it that the smartest people mostly missed that point?" Brannon has concluded that "by nature all people are of both sexes. So that marriage and the bed is not all by any means. The proof? Real youth and old age" (103).

He is troubled, nonetheless, by his ambiguous sexuality. There are times when he wishes that "Mick and Baby were his kids" and that he was their mother (103). Brannon's sister-in-law, Lucille Wilson, insists that he would have made a good mother, and after his wife dies (in part 2), he imagines himself adopting a little girl with "round cheeks and gray eyes and flaxen hair" and sewing dresses for her of "pink crêpe de Chine" with "dainty smocking at the yoke and sleeves." The café owner's desire for omniscience is evident throughout the novel. He sees himself, also, as the adoptive father of a dark-haired little boy who walks at his heels and copies everything he does. The imaginary children think of him as "Our Father" and come to him with questions that they are sure he can answer (180).[16]

Mick's father is a watch repairman who sits at home in a world of imagined business that is clouded by alcohol. "I got so much work to do I don't know where to begin," he tells Mick, with whom he longs to communicate, despite his being unable to make a meaningful connection. Her mother is too busy trying to satisfy the demands of her paying boarders to provide emotional nourishment for her children. Portia Copeland, the family's black servant, tries, but is equally incapable of meeting their needs.[17] Because of their parents' preoccupations, the two younger Kelly children depend on Mick for their routine care and entertainment, while Mick, in turn, remains aloof from her two older sisters, whom she resents. When her sister Etta tells her that she is sick of seeing her wear "those silly boy's clothes," Mick retorts: "I don't want to be like either of you. . . . I'd rather be a boy any day, and I wish I could move in with Bill" (33). Mick's brother Bill (who has outgrown his sister and become obsessed by his own sense of freakishness) lets her keep her drawings and paintings in his room since she has no room—or closet—of her own. Mick's pictures reflect her view of the world as a chaotic and unreasonable place in which she does not fit. They are full of people whose bodies are distorted and who behave irrationally or flee for their lives.[18]

Mick longs for a piano and thinks that nothing is as good as music. "If we had a piano I'd practice every single night and learn every piece in the world," she vows. She tries to develop a musical score on paper, secretly spends her lunch money on piano lessons, and tries to fashion a violin from the bridge of a broken one and a cracked ukulele. Mick swings like a pendulum between dreams and reality, and her every venture into the real world in which a dream is at stake ends unhappily. Symptomatic of her distress is a song that she wanted to compose entitled "This Thing I Want, I Know Not What," but she could not write the song itself. McCullers made explicit in her outline of the novel that music is for Mick a "symbol of beauty and freedom."[19] To see snow—like music, a symbol of escape for Mick—becomes her great urgency. Ironically, snow is the defining image when she loses her virginity to Harry Minowitz.

Mick's simplistic world consists of her private "inside room" (filled with thoughts of John Singer, music, snow, and distant lands) and her "outside room" (in which she reflects on school, family, and her immediate environment, including Singer, whom she bids at will into both rooms). She pictures Singer in a long white sheet in much the way that she imagines God, yet admits that she does not believe in God any more than she does in Santa Claus. Singer is baffled by Mick's apparent devotion, but in his passivity is powerless to repudiate it. He asks nothing of her or of the others and makes no commitment. He is their illusion. Critics have been quick to suggest that Singer is a "false god" to everyone but Brannon, who has seen through him from the beginning.[20] McCullers implied throughout the novel that each character must be responsible for himself alone, and in the novel she made explicit her conviction that man's tendency to create a personal God inevitably results in an inferior creation.[21]

Vital to Mick's maturation and self-awareness are her prom party, her loss of innocence, and, ultimately, the death of Singer. A year after the opening of the narrative (the novel spans fourteen months), Mick teeters on the brink of change and laments that she is not a "member of a bunch." In an attempt to remedy the situation, she gives a prom party and invites twenty of her new classmates at Vocational High, but the event goes awry when it is raided by the younger children of the neighborhood. Mick's guests join the interlopers in their wild antics, a disruption that foreshadows her sexual initiation a few weeks later (the teenaged boys at the party chase the girls with the spine-tipped leaves of Yucca plants—Spanish bayonets—growing in the neighborhood, an image fraught with Freudian overtones).[22] In her outline of the novel, McCullers insisted that the sexual encounter between Mick and Harry after their naked swim in the country "be treated with extreme reticence" since both were "stunned by a sense of evil."[23] In the novel, Harry—a virgin, too—tries to take the blame for their encounter and offers to marry Mick. However, she tells him that she will never marry "with any boy," and Harry runs away that night to Birmingham (210).[24]

Mick's haven, the "inside room" of her imagination, breaks down when Singer commits suicide. She tries to convince herself that her dime store job is temporary, yet knows that she is trapped into womanhood and servitude without choice and has no one to "take it out on" (269). Similarly, she feels cheated by the loss of her virginity, but does not blame it on Harry; it simply happened. The sense of being "cheated" without opportunity for recourse runs as a leitmotif throughout *The Heart Is a Lonely Hunter,* a misfortune that plagues every major character, as well as Mick's younger brother Bubber (who shoots another child in the head with his father's rifle), Dr. Copeland's son William (who loses his legs in the penitentiary), Mick's father (who was a carpenter until disabled from a fall), and several other secondary figures in the novel. Only Biff Brannon and Portia Copeland survive without lamentations of fraud or swindle.

For Singer, the death of Antonapoulos is the ultimate deceit. When Singer travels to another state to visit his friend and learns that he has died, he returns vacantly to his hotel and tries to play the slot machine in the lobby, but it jams, and he is enraged at being "cheated." Although Singer gets his coin back, he recognizes that he has lost his chance to win, just as his friend is forever lost to him. As though to seek redress, Singer steals from his room the towels, soap, toilet paper, a pen, a bottle of ink, and a Bible, his behavior reminiscent of Antonapoulos's wanton shoplifting. The jammed slot machine and Singer's ineffectual response serve as an apt metaphor for his misery upon discovering that Antonapoulos—his personal savior figure—is dead.

Again and again in her fiction, McCullers depicts an inchoate world in which its people are haplessly caught. Their search for wholeness is unsuccessful because their capricious Creator has "withdrawn His hand too soon" (as Big Mama, the mother of Honey Brown, explains it in McCullers's next full-length novel, *The Member of the Wedding*). Because their deity has failed them, they invariably come up with other gods (self-images) of their own. Important to the author's treatment of "homemade gods" in *The Heart Is a Lonely Hunter* is Singer's dream depicting a spiritual hierarchy of gods that collapses and foreshadows his own fall.[25] Each major character appears kneeling in Singer's dream, just as Singer himself kneels before the disinterested Greek. Whereas all of Singer's satellites are disciples of sorts, taking their text from him and feeling abandoned, cheated, by his suicide, Singer thinks only of Antonapoulos and is incapable of living without him.

Similarly, Jake Blount feels betrayed by the mute's suicide as he remembers "all the innermost thoughts that he had told to Singer, and with his death it seemed to him that they were lost. . . . He had given Singer everything and then the man had killed himself. So he was left out on a limb" (260, 263). Blount, too, suffers from the inability to communicate or even to find a common sentiment. Obsessed with one idea—social justice and equality—he hates the inequities in the working conditions of the victimized mill workers whom he tries to incite to strike for higher wages and better working conditions. Their indifference and hostility toward him confirm his sense of powerlessness.

Blount's dreams mirror his frustration. In one, he walks through a starved, silent crowd with a large covered basket ("the burden he had carried in his arms so long" [265]) that he cannot put down. His compulsive monologues convince Brannon that he is "a man thrown off his track by something. . . . Talk—talk—talk. The words came out of his throat like a cataract" (14). Despite his first impression, insists Brannon, Blount is not a freak: "It was like something was deformed about him—but when you looked at him closely each part of him was normal and as it ought to be" (17).[26]

Dr. Benedict Mady Copeland, too, is an alien in a strange land. Born in the South but educated in the North, he has returned to Georgia to rear his family and to lead his people out of sickness and servitude. He dreams day and night of racial equality, but blames his own race for most of its problems. When his daughter Portia tells him that her brother William and many others of their race have been swindled by a black con artist, he replies, "The Negro race of its own accord climbs up on the cross on every Friday" (60). A disciple of Marx and Spinoza, Copeland had named his children for them and planned their lives according to his dreams, but they are grown when the novel begins, and not one has followed the career he dictated. Portia tells him that a "person can't pick up they children and just squeeze them to which-a-way they wants them to be" (61). He must not, in effect, try to play God, she insists. Like Blount at the peak of his frustrations, the doctor abuses himself physically, drinks strong liquor, and hammers his head upon the floor. At the family reunion, he sits alone, angry and frustrated, as the others listen to his father-in-law's discourse on Resurrection Day, when they will be made "white as cotton" (114). Also like Blount, Copeland is plagued by an inability to communicate and to cope with his moral isolation and estrangement from society. When he hears of William's mistreatment in prison and goes to the courthouse to see the judge, he is accused of being drunk and is ridiculed, beaten, and thrown into a crowded, filthy jail that mirrors everything he abhors about the conditions of his own race. Finally, dying of tuberculosis, Copeland retreats to the family farm, wondering, as he lies in his father-in-law's wagon, how it was possible that "all remained to be done and nothing was completed." Although he cannot pull himself upright to talk, he feels the "fire of justice" alive within his disease-ridden body and vows to return "after only a month or two," unwilling to relinquish his illusions (255).

Ultimately, it is the androgynous Brannon who best expresses McCullers's own feelings when he sits alone in his café and is startled by a vision of the power of love and the inevitability of isolation and despair:

> In a swift radiance of illumination he saw a glimpse of human struggle and of valor. Of the endless fluid passage of humanity through endless time. And of those who labor and of those who—one

> word—love. His soul expanded. But for the moment only. For in him he felt a warning, a shaft of terror. Between the two worlds he was suspended. He saw that he was looking at his own face in the counter glass before him. . . . The left eye delved narrowly into the past while the right gazed wide and affrighted into a future of blackness, error, and ruin. And he was suspended between radiance and darkness. Between bitter irony and faith (273).

Brannon is not allowed a total vision, however. He accepts that he will never again love just one person—but "anybody decent who [comes] in out of the street to sit for an hour and have a drink"—yet he represses full knowledge. To know more is to know too much, Brannon concludes. Unlike Singer, Brannon accepts and endures his suffering. Brannon, rather than Singer, emerges as the Christ figure. It is with Brannon in a tableau of affirmation that seems frozen in time that McCullers closes her novel.

Upon publication of *The Heart Is a Lonely Hunter* on June 4, 1940, early reviewers greeted the book and its young author with high praise. Rose Feld, writing for the *New York Times Book Review,* observed that McCullers had "an astonishing perception of humanity," and that her imagination was "rich and fearless."[27] Ben Ray Redman declared to readers of *The Saturday Review of Literature* that *The Heart Is a Lonely Hunter* was an extraordinary novel "in its own right, considerations of authorship apart."[28] Richard Wright thought McCullers's quality of despair in the novel was "unique and natural . . . more natural and authentic than that of Faulkner." Wright said that he was impressed most by the "astonishing humanity" that enabled a "white writer, for the first time in Southern fiction, to handle Negro characters with as much ease and justice as those of her own race."[29] The subject of numerous critical studies over the nearly fifty years since its publication, *The Heart Is a Lonely Hunter* remains, in the opinion of many critics, one of only a handful of truly distinguished first novels by major American writers of the twentieth century.

Notes

1. Whit Burnett also bought a second tale, "Like That," which remained unpublished until McCullers's sister included it in the posthumous collection, *The Mortgaged Heart*, ed. Margarita G. Smith (Boston: Houghton Mifflin, 1971), 64–73.

2. For another version of McCullers's illumination regarding the transformation of Harry Minowitz into John Singer, see McCullers's essay, "The Flowering Dream: Notes on Writing," *Esquire* 52 (Dec. 1959): 162–164; reprinted in *The Mortgaged Heart*, 275. This version is part of an unpublished manuscript identified only as "A speech on her first public appearance." Oliver Evans Collection, Humanities Research Center, University of Texas, Austin.

3. Virginia Spencer Carr, *The Lonely Hunter: A Biography of Carson McCullers* (Garden City: Doubleday, 1975), 19.

4. McCullers's working title was "The Mute." The book was retitled *The Heart Is a Lonely Hunter* just before publication upon the insistence of McCullers's editor, Robert Linscott. The new title was taken from a phrase in the poem "The Lonely Hunter" by William Sharp (Fiona MacLeod): "But my heart is a lonely hunter that hunts / on a lonely hill." See Fiona MacLeod, *Poems and Dramas* (New York: Duffield, 1914), 27.

5. Carson McCullers, "Author's Outline of 'The Mute' " in Oliver Evans, *Carson McCullers: Her Life and Work* (London: Peter Owen, 1965), 195–215; further citations to "Author's Outline of 'The Mute' " are from the *The Mortgaged Heart*, 124–149.

6. Ralph McGill, *The South and the Southerner* (Boston: Little, Brown, 1959), 217.

7. "Author's Outline of 'The Mute,' " 124, 148.

8. "Author's Outline of 'The Mute,' " 148.

9. McCullers, *The Heart Is a Lonely Hunter* (Boston: Houghton Mifflin, 1940), 12. All page references within the text are to this edition.

10. Mick's chapters are 1, 5, 9, 11, and 14; Brannon's chapters are 2 and 8; Copeland's chapters are 3, 6, 10, and 13; Blount's chapters are 4 and 12; Singer's chapters are 7 and 15.

11. "Author's Outline of 'The Mute,' " 138.

12. Barbara A. Farrelly, "*The Heart Is a Lonely Hunter*: A Literary Symphony," *Pembroke Magazine* 20 (1988): 16–23.

13. "Author's Outline of 'The Mute,' " 137.

14. In Thomas Ryan's screenplay of *The Heart Is a Lonely Hunter*, Brannon was eliminated as a major character on the grounds that he was the "least dramatizable in the book." Thomas Ryan to Carr, letter, 8 Oct. 1970.

15. McCullers herself was thirteen when she began smoking, convinced that if her growth rate continued she would be eight feet tall in a matter of months and no different from the freaks who came annually to Columbus, Georgia, with the midway of the Chattahoochee Valley Fair. Carr, *The Lonely Hunter*, 30.

16. Although Brannon plays the role of parent only in his fantasies, there are, in fact, many actual fathers and mothers portrayed in McCullers's later fiction. Yet not one exerts any positive influence upon his or her children. Some are dead (through childbirth or suicide); the rest are either passive and weak or too concerned with gaining identity and personal fulfillment through their offspring (or with finding some shred of meaning in their own wasted lives independent of their children) to provide more than the rudiments of a family structure or to demonstrate real affection, compassion, or love. The children repeatedly look elsewhere for someone to fulfill their insatiable needs.

17. Portia Copeland is modeled in part upon Vannie Copland Jackson, a cook in the Smith family household. Vannie Copland Jackson to Carr, interview, Columbus, Ga., 16 Oct. 1987.

18. For an excellent discussion of the child's search for his/her place (and his/her sexual identity) in the adult world, see Louise Westling, "Carson McCullers's Tomboys," *Southern Humanities Review* 4 (1982): 339–350; and Constance M. Perry, "Carson McCullers and the Female *Wunderkind*," *The Southern Literary Journal* 19 [1] (Fall 1986): 36–45.

19. "Author's Outline of 'The Mute,' " 128.

20. See, especially, Frank Durham, "God and No God in *The Heart Is a Lonely Hunter*," *South Atlantic Quarterly* 56 (Autumn 1957): 494–499; Ihab Hassan, "Carson McCullers: The Alchemy of Love and Aesthetics of Pain," *Modern Fiction Studies* 5 (Winter 1959–60): 311–321; Wayne D. Dodd, "The Development of Theme Through Symbol in the Novels of Carson McCullers," *Georgia Review* 17 (Summer 1963): 206–213; Chester E. Eisinger, *Fiction of the Forties* (Chicago: University of Chicago Press, 1963) 247; Klaus Lubbers, "The Necessary Order: A Study of Theme and Structure in Carson McCullers' Fiction," *Jahrbüch für Amerikastudien* 8 (1963): 187–204; and David Madden, "The Paradox of the Need for Privacy and the Need for Understanding in Carson McCullers's *The Heart Is a Lonely Hunter*," *Literature and Psychology* 17 [2–3] (1967): 128–140.

21. "Author's Outline of 'The Mute,' " 124.

22. See also Irving Buchen, "Carson McCullers: The Case of Convergence," *Bucknell Review* 21 (Spring 1973): 15–28; and Jack B. Moore, "Carson McCullers: The Heart Is a Timeless Hunter," *Twentieth Century Literature* 11 (July 1965): 76–81.

23. "Author's Outline of 'The Mute,' " 129, 130.

24. Constance Perry (in "Carson McCullers and the Female *Wunderkind*") argues convincingly that Mick's admission that "she was a grown person now, whether she wanted to be or not" (274) marked her recognition that in her culture to be an adult woman was to be inferior, "somehow shameful and obscene" (42–43); Perry concludes that with "the intrusion of adult sexuality into [Mick's] world, she also loses her identity and her artistic dreams."

25. Durham (in "God and No God in *The Heart Is a Lonely Hunter*") treats the novel as an "ironic religious allegory" and sees both Singer and Antonapoulos as Gods who neither understand their suppliants nor communicate with them. Dodd (in "The Development of Theme Through Symbol in the Novels of Carson McCullers") suggests that in McCullers's depiction of an endless progression of gods there is a "pseudo-metaphysical basis" for the "total lack of understanding and communication between man and man." See also Mary A. Whitt, "The Mutes in McCullers's *The Heart Is a Lonely Hunter*," *Pembroke Magazine* 20 (1988): 24–29. Whitt addresses the roles of the two deaf mutes and analyzes the religious overtones apparent in the "godless" society in which the characters of this novel live.

26. See Frances Kestler, "Gothic Influence of the Grotesque Characters of the Lonely Hunter," *Pembroke Magazine* 20 (1988): 30–36.

27. Rose Feld, "A Remarkable First Novel of Lonely Lives," *New York Times Book Review* (16 June 1940): 6.

28. Ben Ray Redman, "Of Human Loneliness," *The Saturday Review of Literature* 22 (8 June 1940): 6.

29. Richard Wright, "Inner Landscape," *New Republic*, 103 (5 Aug. 1940): 195.

CHAPTER THREE

Reflections in a Golden Eye

McCullers's second novel had its genesis in the arrest of a young soldier, a voyeur, who was caught outside the married officers' quarters at Fort Bragg, North Carolina, during the time that the author was living with her husband in nearby Fayetteville. McCullers remembered, too, a murder trial in Columbus, Georgia, in which an enlisted man at Fort Benning was convicted of killing his commanding officer. These two incidents, coupled with her recent reading of Freud and of D. H. Lawrence's *The Prussian Officer and Other Stories*, contributed to the creation of setting, plot, and characterization in *Reflections in a Golden Eye*, and especially to her depiction of the brilliant, neurotic Captain Penderton and the unsophisticated, almost moronic Private Williams, to whom the Captain is attracted.

McCullers told her editor that writing the book "for fun" was as easy as "eating candy" and that she had written it in scarcely two months as therapeutic diversion from her impoverished and unhappy life in Fayetteville.[1] But she did not think her tale publishable, and in correspondence with friends during this period she spoke of it as her fairy tale in which everything was done "very lightly." The story practically wrote itself, she said. She had no idea what her characters were going to do until they did it.[2]

George Davis, literary editor of *Harper's Bazaar*, discovered her strange, evocative tale while rummaging through a batch of pieces she had put aside in a dresser drawer in the old brownstone they shared in Brooklyn Heights. Impressed by her first novel, Davis pushed for other manuscripts to publish in his magazine and insisted that her army post tale would fit nicely into two installments in *Harper's Bazaar*. Its title was changed from "Army Post" to *Reflections in a Golden Eye* when the manuscript was published in hard cover on February 14, 1941.

Most of the characters in *Reflections in a Golden Eye* are grotesques. They manifest no physical deformities (Alison Langdon, who cuts off the nipples of her breasts with garden shears, is the sole exception), but they are maimed emotionally. Throughout the author's canon, freakishness is a symbol of a character's sense of alienation, of his being trapped within a single identity without the possibility of a meaningful connection with anyone else. In the preface to a paperback reissue in 1950, playwright Tennessee Williams called *Reflections in a Golden Eye* "one of the purest and most powerful of those works which are conceived in that Sense of The Awful which is the desperate black root of nearly all significant modern art."[3] Critics in general agree that this book is the author's most deterministic and pessimistic tale.

In "The Flowering Dream: Notes on Writing," an essay published twenty years later, McCullers declared that "one cannot explain accusations of morbidity. A writer can only say he writes from the seed which flowers later in the subconscious. . . . Anything that pulses and moves and walks around the room, no matter what thing it is doing, is natural and human to a writer."[4] She said that she becomes so immersed in her characters that their motives become her own. "I become the characters I write about and I bless the Latin poet Terence who said, 'Nothing human is alien to me,' " she insisted. To McCullers, it was love, "especially love of a person who is incapable of returning or receiving it," that lay at the heart of her selection of grotesque figures with whom she peopled much of her fictional landscape.[5] She viewed the denial of love—a human choice—as the basest evil within man's capabilities.

A much shorter work than McCullers's first novel, *Reflections in a Golden Eye* totals seventy pages of narrative and is divided into four sections. The first several sentences of the tale establish the setting and narrative tone in a manner not unlike the opening paragraph of *The Heart Is a Lonely Hunter*: "An Army Post in peacetime is a dull place. Things happen, but then they happen over and over again." The general plan of the fort with its "huge concrete barracks, the neat rows of officers' homes built one precisely like the others" reinforces the repetitiveness that pervades the novel. "But perhaps the dullness of a post is caused most of all by insularity and by a surfeit of leisure and safety," McCullers continues, "for once a man enters the army he is expected only to follow the heels ahead of him."[6] Yet things "do occasionally happen on an army post that are not likely to re-occur" (3). Having established a mood of monotonous regularity in an encapsulated environment, McCullers's omniscient narrator continues by sharpening the reader's focus and preparing him for the extraordinary action to follow: "There is a fort in the South where a few years ago a murder was committed. The participants of this tragedy were: two officers, a soldier, two women, a Filipino, and a horse" (3).

The narrator's detachment from the action itself and the clean, bare prose with which he (or she, for McCullers in no way discloses the gender of her narrator) tells the story impose an ironic sense of understatement upon the tragedy that ensues. In his recounting of the story, the narrator shifts points of view as he empathizes with the two major characters (in their "caught" condition of spiritual isolation) and, from time to time, with the lesser ones in a fashion similar to the narrative style of *The Heart Is a Lonely Hunter*. Nature imposes itself, also, upon the characters in *Reflections in a Golden Eye* in the mode of gothic romance and contributes to the deterministic elements of the novel. The story is played against light and dark, and the showy colors of autumn give way quickly to the cold and oppressive wind of winter as the tale darkens and deepens. Private Ellgee Williams seems protected by the sun and derives his strength from it, but he is vulnerable, his loss of innocence imminent, when he ventures into the night. Chance thrusts him into a twilight encounter with a nude woman, whereupon he is drawn irrevocably into a Dantean circle of wooded shadows, night, and death.

Until he views the nude Leonora Penderton, Private Williams has worn the "strange, rapt face of a Gauguin primitive" (32), his eyes without expression. Reared in an all-male household and trained to believe women to be carriers of a horrible disease, Williams has "never willingly touched, or looked at, or spoken to a female" since he was a small child (13). Yet he has been attracted to animals since the age of seventeen when he bought a cow and milked her with "soft urgent whispers" and pressed his forehead against her flank as though they were lovers (20). When the story opens, Williams has been in the army for two years and is assigned to the stables. The narrator observes that the other stablehands "would think it strange" if they could see him standing for long hours with his arms around the neck of a pregnant mare and caressing her swollen belly. Rapt in a world of animals and nature, Private Ellgee Williams is so removed from civilization that he is, appropriately, amoral.

Captain Weldon Penderton, depicted by McCullers as one of civilization's "commodities," is so spiritually isolated from his fellow creatures that his only connection or exit lies in violence or death. Like Biff Brannon in his impotence and spiritual isolation, the Captain is drawn to his wife's lovers. Leonora Penderton, the Captain's wife, fears "neither man, beast, nor the devil" (11). The uninhibited woman is voluptuous, beautiful, narcissistic, and simpleminded. She drinks her rye whiskey straight, dreams of well-stuffed turkeys, and is passionate about two things: her headstrong chestnut stallion, Firebird, and sex (she has been faithful to her lover, the Major, for two years). Leonora is admired by the other officers' wives on the base as an entertaining hostess and sportswoman whose wit and other attributes compensate handily for deficiencies of intellect.

When Penderton tells his wife, upon her return from the stables, that she looks like a slattern for lounging downstairs without her shoes or boots and asks if she intends to sit down to dinner with the Langdons in such fashion, she replies, "And why not, you old prissy?" (10) Then, to taunt him further, she strips herself naked before going upstairs to dress.[7] Penderton follows her to the foot of the stairs and threatens to kill her for her impudence, whereupon she squelches him again. "Son, have you ever been collared and dragged out in the street and thrashed by a naked woman?" she asks (10). What neither knows is that the Private has just finished his work detail in the yard outside their home and, having witnessed the entire scenario, stands entranced at the window. Just as the Captain has been vaguely attracted to the Major, so, too, is he disquieted by a growing awareness of his aversion to the Private.

The scene now set, the action ensues with calculated intensity, while a macabre humor combines the horrible with the ridiculous. Juxtaposed with these three characters (who are referred to most often by the narrator as the Captain, the Private, and the Lady) is another trio: the Major, Alison (the Major's wife), and Anacleto (their houseboy).

Major Langdon, predictably voracious in every activity (eating, drinking, gambling, riding, and fornicating), is the least interesting character in the novel. He is good-natured and gets along well with the enlisted men and his fellow officers, but any emotional fulfillment in his marriage had been destroyed by the birth of his deformed, only child, Catherine (now dead), whom he loathed and could not bear to hold. For years the Major's delicate wife has suffered from heart disease, and the child's death has brought her to the brink of lunacy. Compounding these physical and psychological weaknesses is Alison's knowledge of her husband's affair with Leonora and her own desperate attraction to Leonora (an attachment that quickly played itself out). At the opening of the novel, Alison hates her husband and has distanced herself from everyone but the spritelike Anacleto, whom she brought with her from the Philippines when he was seventeen. Anacleto worships his mistress and attends her constantly, having matched her "wail for wail" in the labor room, and now he regularly tastes her medicine and behaves in almost every activity as a mirror image. Despite the marked differences between Anacleto's chatter and Alison's measured and composed speech, their voices and enunciation sound "so precisely alike that they [seem] to be softly echoing each other" (29). At night when she awakens fearful and upset, he holds her hand, his face wearing "the same sickly grimace as her own" (57). His habit on such occasions is to bring her hot Ovaltine and build a fire on the bedroom hearth, then to spread out his watercolors and paint while she tells him every detail of the nightmare that has shattered her sleep.

The title *Reflections in a Golden Eye* comes from an incident in the novel that occurs in the twilight hours of one such night as Anacleto sits painting beside his mistress. As he stares into the embers of the fire, he exclaims: "Look! A peacock of a sort of ghastly green. With one immense golden eye. And in these reflections of something tiny and—" "Grotesque," she answers, finishing his thought (59).

Similarly, reflections figure prominently throughout the novel. Like Leonora, Anacleto is a narcissist and cannot pass a mirror without looking at himself. He fancies himself a ballet dancer and asks after performing a little dance in Alison's bedroom, "Have you ever noticed how well 'Bravo' and 'Anacleto' go together?" (30). McCullers's concept of a Creator whose specialty is freaks emerges in the novel as Anacleto observes that "the Lord had blundered grossly in the making of everyone except himself and Madame Alison—the sole exceptions to this were people behind footlights, midgets, great artists, and such-like fabulous folk" (28).

In the fourth and final section of the novel, Alison's tenuous hold on reality gives way at last. During her second night in a mental hospital she dies of a heart attack and Anacleto disappears. Upon Alison's death—which has caused the Major "more shame than grief"—each character undergoes significant change (76). The Major appears stunned and helpless, speaks piously of his deceased wife, and makes "doleful platitudes concerning God, the soul, suffering, and death" (76). Leonora treats him with "vacant sweetness" and goes alone to the movies. Her body appears to have "lost some of its youthful muscularity," and to the Captain, it seems that "in some mysterious way the lives of all three of them had come to a close" (79).

It is in this mood and under these circumstances that Penderton takes no heart in his usual malicious gossip until the Major observes that the army "might have made a man" of Anacleto and "knocked all the nonsense out of him" (77). As though with sudden illumination, Penderton asks the Major: "You mean that any fulfillment obtained at the expense of normalcy is wrong, and should not be allowed to bring happiness. In short, it is better, because it is morally honorable, for the square peg to keep scraping about the round hole rather than to discover and use the unorthodox square that would fit it?" (77).

What the other characters in McCullers's tale have no way of knowing is that Penderton sees himself as they see Anacleto: the "square peg" scraping about the round hole in an imperfect fit rather than discovering and using the "unorthodox square that would fit it." Almost everything about the Captain is out-of-round, discordant. His ambivalent emotions reveal themselves early in the novel when he paces restlessly in his study, unable to work, at which point McCullers's narrator observes that there are "times when a man's greatest need is to have someone to love, some focal point for his diffused emotions. Also there are times when the irritations, disappointments, and fears of life, restless as spermatozoids, must be released in hate. The unhappy Captain had no one to hate and for the past months he had been miserable" (33).

Although Penderton is afraid of horses, he rides regularly because it "was another one of his ways of tormenting himself" (47). When he takes Firebird out without his wife's knowledge and torments him by letting him run short distances, then checking him without warning, the animal bolts and the Captain is certain that he will be killed. Then a new and wild feeling takes over, and "having given up life, the Captain suddenly began to live" (49). The world becomes a kaleidoscope, and each of the multiple visions impress themselves upon him with "burning vividness":

> On the ground half-buried in the leaves there was a little flower, dazzling white and beautifully wrought. A thorny pine cone, the flight of a bird in the blue windy sky, a fiery shaft of sunshine in the green gloom—these the Captain saw as though for the first time in his life. He was conscious of the pure keen air and he felt the marvel of his own tense body, his laboring heart, and the miracle of blood, muscle, nerves, and bone. The Captain knew no terror now; he had soared to the rare level of consciousness where the mystic feels that the earth is he and that he is the earth (49).

At the height of his wild ride, it occurs to Penderton that the beast is giving out, and he experiences a new dread, that he will not die. Like McCullers's characters in *The Heart Is a Lonely Hunter* who feel cheated, so, too, does Penderton feel swindled out of what is rightfully his, and he beats the horse savagely. His anger still unappeased, he drops sobbing to the ground and passes out. When he regains consciousness, he discovers Private Williams standing over him, nude, having witnessed the ruthless beating. Then a new rush of emotion—hatred—becomes "as exorbitant as the joy he had experienced on runaway Firebird," and his "mind [swarms] with a dozen cunning schemes by which he could make the soldier suffer" (51). Having lived a rigid and unemotional life, wedded to discipline, public opinion, and the regimentation of army life, the Captain does not question this strange hatred. He takes triple doses of Seconal that send him, ultimately, into deep slumber and voluptuous sensations.

Penderton's affirmation, a recognition of his true being, comes too late to restrict the inexorable flow of events that sweep him to his destruction. Meanwhile, Williams, too, is unalterably affected. Until he saw the nude Leonora walking catlike through her living room, he was content; but just as the Captain has been inexplicably drawn to him, so, too, is he drawn to her. He fears her nakedness, yet is attracted to it, the sight of the Lady's body having initiated a chain of events unlike anything the soldier has ever known. Each night he keeps a silent vigil at her home: first, outside the window of the Captain's study; then, in her room, where he watches Leonora as she sleeps. Like an animal, he crouches by her bed, examines her perfumes, touches a strand of her bronze hair, and holds a piece of her clothing on his lap. The memories of his nightly vigils are relentless and sensual: the thick rug, the silk spread, the scent of perfume, the "soft luxurious warmth of woman-flesh, the quiet darkness—the alien sweetness in his heart and the tense power in his body as he crouched there near to her. Once having known this he could not let it go; in him was engendered a dark, drugged craving as certain of fulfillment as death" (83). Paradoxically, while the Private is being drawn to destruction through his attraction to Leonora, the Captain is being overwhelmed by a feeling that, according to the narrator, "both repelled and fascinated him—it was as though he and the young soldier were wrestling together naked, body to body, in a fight to death" (53).

Williams's seventh visit to Leonora's bedside is his last. The Captain detects the Private's silhouette in his wife's room, loads his pistol, crosses the hall, and switches on the light. He shoots twice, leaving "one raw hole" in the soldier's chest. Leonora is only half awake when Major Langdon, having heard the shots, enters the house, hurries up the stairs, and finds the Captain "slumped against the wall," dressed in a "queer, coarse wrapper," looking like a "broken and dissipated monk." Even in death, Private Williams retains "the look of warm, animal comfort," his grave face unchanged, his "palms upward on the carpet as though in sleep" (85).

Just as Penderton has his one rare moment of illumination, so, too, does Private Williams, who reaches (through Leonora) a state of human consciousness and recognizes the need to belong. The civilized world is too sinister for the young initiate, however, and he is killed by the Captain before he has an opportunity to come to terms with his newly discovered identity. The Private remains the Gauguin primitive, the child who is forever suspended between innocence and experience, unable to grapple with his expulsion from Eden.

Although McCullers's chilling tale is starkly devoid of any relief through music or music imagery, a subtle kind of mirror counterpoint runs throughout in the dissonant/harmonic relationship between the five characters and the horse, all inextricably unified, yet developed with linear individuality. Whereas in counterpoint, two dissimilar themes or melodies run counter, yet concurrently, and combine eventually into a harmonious whole, in this dissonant tale the chords are too harsh, the melody too broken to ever result in anything more than scattered musical strains.

Had fate not willed it otherwise, the Captain might have been a private, too (just as he fancied himself in his pursuit of Private Ellgee Williams). As the square peg in the round hole, the Captain's life had been determined for him, first by his family, then by the Major Langdons in his career. The self-estranged Captain is fated to die the isolate, having severed his one tenuous grasp at communion with another human being.[8]

Many contemporary reviewers of the novel chastised McCullers for what they saw as her obsessive preoccupation with abnormality, her unsympathetic and preposterous characters, and her "inversions and mutilations and nastiness" that "stick in the mind like burrs."[9] Although Rose Feld of *The New York Herald Tribune* thought the novel superior to *The Heart Is a Lonely Hunter* in its compression and careful construction, she regretted McCullers's "lapse of taste" in allowing a character to mutilate her breasts (an incident "as physically unnerving to the reader as anything that has appeared in print," said Feld) and she was convinced that the author's having "matched Faulkner in his morbidity" added nothing to "her power as an artist."[10] Basil Davenport called the tale a "viper's knot of neurasthenic relationships among characters whom the author seems hardly to comprehend," yet admitted to his readers of *The Saturday Review* that she wrote with a "haunting power and suggestiveness" that could be felt instantly.[11] Reviewers in general agreed that McCullers's second novel fell short of the promise of the first. Otis Ferguson stood practically alone among contemporary critics in his assessment for readers of *The New Republic,* stating that the novel was a "brilliant piece of execution, hard, exact and graceful in likeness, a sort of cameo in fiction."[12] Tennessee Williams insisted that *Reflections in a Golden Eye* was a better novel than *The Heart is a Lonely Hunter,* finding in it the "one attribute which had yet to be shown in Carson McCullers's stunning array of gifts: the gift of mastery over a youthful lyricism."[13]

Notes

1. Carson McCullers to Robert Linscott, undated letter, from Robert Linscott Collection, Washington University Libraries, St. Louis, Mo.

2. Carson McCullers to Robert Linscott, undated letter, from Robert Linscott Collection, Washington University Libraries, St. Louis, Mo.; also McCullers to Louis Untermeyer, undated letter, from Louis Untermeyer Private Collection, Newton, Conn.

3. Tennessee Williams, "Introduction," *Reflections in a Golden Eye* (New York: Bantam, 1950), xiv.

4. Carson McCullers, "The Flowering Dream: Notes on Writing," *Esquire* 52 (Dec. 1959): 162–164; reprinted in Carson McCullers, *The Mortgaged Heart* (Boston: Houghton Mifflin, 1971), 276–277.

5. "The Flowering Dream," in *The Mortgaged Heart*, 274.

6. Arleen Portada, "Sex-Role Rebellion and the Failure of Marriage in the Fiction of Carson McCullers," *Pembroke Magazine* 20 (1988): 63–71. Portada observes that "it is hard to say what is truly 'abnormal' in this novel, since the characters, bizarre though their actions might be, are set in such an unnatural environment."

7. Alfred Kazin, *Bright Book of Life: American Novelists and Storytellers from Hemingway to Mailer* (Boston: Atlantic Monthly Press and Little, Brown, 1971), 53. Kazin attributes to McCullers the "intuition that human beings could be in psychic states so absolute and self-contained that they repelled each other sexually."

8. Donna Bauerly, "Themes of Eros and Agape in the Major Fiction of Carson McCullers," *Pembroke Magazine* 20 (1988): 72–76. Bauerly's insightful essay traces how "every movement away from Love of Eros is frustrated" in this bleak novel in which the characters "cannot develop even a small capacity for true concern for anyone other than themselves."

9. Robert Littell, *The Yale Review* 30 (Mar. 1941): xii–xiv. See also Clifton Fadiman, *The New Yorker* 17 (15 Feb. 1941): 78–80; and Fred T. Marsh, "At an Army Post," *New York Times Book Review* (2 Mar. 1941): 6.

10. Rose Feld, *New York Herald Tribune Books* (16 Feb. 1941): 8.

11. Basil Davenport, *Saturday Review* 23 (22 Feb. 1941): 12.

12. Otis Ferguson, "Fiction: Odd and Ordinary," *The New Republic* 114 (3 Mar. 1941): 317. See also Margaret Marshall, "Masterpiece at 24" *Time* 37 (17 Feb. 1941): 96.

13. Tennessee Williams, "Introduction," *Reflections in a Golden Eye* (New York: Bantam, 1950), xiv.

CHAPTER FOUR

The Ballad of the Sad Café

The monotony and boredom that permeated the author's life with her husband in 1939 before their move from Fayetteville, North Carolina, contributed not only to the completion of *Reflections in a Golden Eye,* but also to her novella, *The Ballad of the Sad Café,* published for the first time in 1943 in a single issue of *Harper's Bazaar.*[1] More important to the story line of the tale than McCullers's southern discomfort, however, was her predicament in New York in 1940 and 1941. She had hoped for a committed relationship with her new friend Annemarie Clarac-Schwarzenbach, having fallen deeply in love with her, but it became apparent to McCullers soon after their involvement that nothing further would develop.

To suffer in despair was her destiny as a mortal, she reasoned, turning once more to fiction to express what she saw as her truths. Although McCullers had been working for many months on a manuscript that she referred to as "The Bride and Her Brother," its design and technique had not yet revealed themselves to her (a metaphysical experience McCullers described later as "the grace of labor").[2] She realized while in the nurturing environment of her native Columbus that she could put off no longer the strange tale of thwarted love that had grown out of her tangled relationships with her husband and her Swiss friend. That winter she wrote her editor (Robert Linscott) that passion and tension in her life were necessary if she were to write at all, but that she needed it in smaller doses. With her husband, there had been too much tension, and passion had been replaced by disillusionment, ennui, and disgust. But now, removed physically from the two people with whom she had been most deeply involved, she found herself writing well once more. Her new tale was better than anything else she had done, she reported.[3]

McCullers told a number of friends while she was at work on her "folk tale" during the summer of 1941 at Yaddo Artists Colony that she had written the "music" for it years earlier as a result of her experiences with people she loved. Her lyrics, however, were more recently inspired. In the first week of her stay at Yaddo, she became enamored of Katherine Anne Porter, a fellow guest and the reputed grande dame of the colony, a crush that added still another dimension to her tale. According to Porter, McCullers lost no time in making her infatuation known and followed her about the colony in the very manner in which the characters she was creating moon over one another in *The Ballad of the Sad Café*.[4]

Although the pivotal character in the tale that McCullers was writing bears a resemblance to any number of individuals in her life (and even, to some extent, to the author herself), Cousin Lymon owes his creation, in part, to an actual hunchback whom McCullers saw in a Sand Street bar that she frequented in Brooklyn Heights when she lived at 7 Middagh Street, near the old Brooklyn Naval Yard. In her essay "Brooklyn Is My Neighborhood," McCullers described him as "a little hunchback who struts in proudly every evening, and is petted by everyone, given free drinks, and treated as a sort of mascot by the proprietor."[5] But even more relevant to his development as a character was McCullers's wry humor and sheer delight in reading and hearing recounted tales of folk epic and classical mythology, as well as of bizarre situations found within her contemporary world. Mary A. Gervin has written convincingly of certain "frames of reference" and mythic parallels between Amelia/Macy and Artemis/Orion.[6]

Still another situation in McCullers's life found its way into her tale that summer, too: her abandonment by Reeves and his love affair with their best friend, David Diamond. McCullers wrote Diamond from Yaddo when she finished her "strange fairy tale," as she repeatedly described it, that it was for him. (Diamond, in turn, dedicated his ballet *The Dream of Audubon* to both McCullers and Reeves and set to music her recently published poem, "The Twisted Trinity," yet another handling of her troubled life.)[7] In the fictional tale, Amelia is abandoned by Cousin Lymon—whom she loves inordinately—in favor of Marvin Macy. The two men team up against her, steal her treasures, wreck her café and distillery, and leave town together.

Critic Margaret Walsh has argued cogently that *The Ballad Of the Sad Café* is not a "fairy tale" but an "anti-fairy tale," for "unlike the redeeming love of fairy tales, love in McCullers's tale is the spell that weakens the will, the enchantment that can dwarf giants"; thus to "lay oneself bare to love is to be open to disloyalty, to be meek, powerless, and defenseless, to be at the mercy of love's unpredictability."[8]

The twisted, ill-fated triangles that haunt the lives of McCullers's fictional characters repeatedly haunted the author in reality as well. The theme of abandonment (that had prevailed in *The Heart Is a Lonely Hunter*) is important not only to *The Ballad of the Sad Café,* but even more so to the longer work in progress that summer, the novel that eventually became *The Member of the Wedding*. McCullers finished her novella at Yaddo during the summer of 1941, then put it away for two years, intending to write two more tales of about the same length and to publish them as a trilogy in one volume. Caught up in the writing of *The Member of the Wedding,* however, she never worked on the other tales she envisioned, and *The Ballad of the Sad Café* was published in 1943 in a single issue of *Harper's*

Bazaar. Eight years later, it became the title story in her omnibus collection, *"The Ballad of the Sad Café" and Other Works,* which included all of the long fiction published to date and six of her short stories.

The narrator of McCullers's novella maintains a relatively objective distance from the scene and situation that he (or she) describes in much the same manner as the narrator does in *Reflections in a Golden Eye.* He is not a specific character within any scene, but his commentary and subtle forewarnings function like a Greek chorus. He sees the dangers inherent in the triangle of Amelia, Lymon, and Macy, but is powerless to act. He does not pretend to know everything, but his omniscient voice sets the mood and pace of the action to follow, shifting from formal, stylized, poetic, and at times archaic, to the colorful and colloquial folk patterns of the simple mill people who frequent Miss Amelia's café.

Over the years McCullers's narrator has evoked more critical discussion than has any other aspect of the tale. Robert Rechnitz argued cogently in 1968 that the author's "childlike style" served her especially well in *The Ballad of the Sad Café,* for it enabled the narrator to hide behind a facade of childlike innocence that became a "kind of buffer to fend off what would otherwise be unbearable."[9] A later essay, Dawson F. Gaillard's "The Presence of the Narrator in McCullers' *Ballad of the Sad Café,*" posits that the empathetic presence of the narrator makes it impossible for the reader "to distance himself from the emotional impact of the act," and that it is the oral quality of the tale and the personal balladeer's response to the café that lifts the café to mythic proportions.[10] Critics have generally agreed that the narrator's most striking characteristic is his (or her) compassion for the three principal characters, whose traits are employed by McCullers as symbols of the moral isolation and pain to which one inevitably falls heir in the absence of any kind of meaningful communication with another human being.

Told as one long flashback, the story actually begins at the end. Unlike her first two books with their three- and four-part divisions, *The Ballad of the Sad Café* is tightly compressed into one continuous narrative that relies upon narration alone and an occasional space break to emphasize passage of time or an extraordinary turn of events.

When the reader first encounters Amelia Evans, by far the most pitiful and tragic figure in the tale, she is living alone behind boarded-up windows in a large, sagging house on the main street of a small town in what appears to be the hills of North Georgia. It is August, and "sometimes in the late afternoon when the heat is at its worst a hand will slowly open the shutter and a face will look down on the town. It is a face like the terrible dim faces known in dreams—sexless and white" (1). The solitary Miss Amelia is a freakishly tall, pale woman whose "two gray crossed eyes" are turned so sharply inward that they seem to be exchanging with each other "one long and secret gaze of grief" (1). Amelia is six feet two inches tall and has bones and muscles like a man's. She cares "nothing for the love of men," although she identifies with them in her labors of sausage making, bricklaying, and carpentry. The town's only general practitioner, she doles out her homemade medicines, but is uncomfortable with women and refuses to treat any "female complaint" (12). Like Private Williams in *Reflections in a Golden Eye*, Amelia was reared in a motherless home. She had no idea what might be expected of her in a romantic relationship and had no basis for remorse over her violent expulsion of Marvin Macy from the bridal bedchamber or of her abuse of him later. When Amelia, in turn, is abandoned by Lymon, she evokes the townspeople's pity.

The town itself is dreary and undistinguished, for "not much is there except the cotton mill, the two-room houses where the workers live, a few peach trees, a church with two colored windows, and a miserable main street only a hundred yards long. On Saturdays the tenants from the nearby farms come in for a day of talk and trade. Otherwise the town is lonesome, sad, and like a place that is far off and estranged from all other places in the world" (1). Nature imposes itself upon the hapless people with short, raw winters and summers that are "white with glare and fiery hot" (1). In such a godforsaken place, the "soul rots with boredom" (53), and one's only relief, suggests the balladeer, is "to walk down the Forks Falls Road and listen to the chain gang" (1).

In the process of telling his tale, the narrator overcomes his boredom and, as critic John McNally has carefully demonstrated, adds a meaningful dimension to his own banal existence.[11] But the town was once quite different, and so was Amelia, insists the narrator. In addition to having been the richest woman in town, she also ran the only local general store and made the best liquor in the county from an illegal still deep in the nearby swamp. Obviously displeased over the state of affairs in the community, she was ill at ease with the rest of the townspeople because they could not "be taken into the hands and changed overnight to something more worthwhile and profitable" (2). Amelia's indifference to others was seen most clearly in her strange, ten-day unconsummated marriage to Macy, whom she drove out of her house—and out of town—after getting him to turn over all of his worldly possessions to her. Macy's humiliation by Amelia caused him to revert fiercely to his old, cruel habits that had shocked the town and gained him notoriety throughout the state. Captured, finally, he was charged for murder and any number of shotgun robberies and sent off to the penitentiary outside of Atlanta.

The narrator explains that some eleven years have passed since that event, however, and that Miss Amelia's independence and meanspiritedness are legendary. Thus the townspeople are amazed beyond belief when a tubercular and repulsive-looking hunchback struts into town one day and claims distant kinship with her. She calls him Cousin Lymon, and overnight he becomes the focus of her world. Lymon looks like a sick pelican with his thin crooked legs, oversized head, and great warped chest, and he is described repeatedly through distasteful bird imagery. For the first time in Amelia's life she feels pity, moved first by his tears, then by love—a love that she offers freely, having intuited that the little hunchback is no threat to her sexuality. Critic Joseph R. Millichap has aptly described Lymon as "a man loved without sex, a child acquired without pain, and a companion" whom Amelia found "more acceptable than a husband or a child."[12]

In one of the most frequently quoted passages from McCullers's entire canon, the narrator addresses mankind (and womankind) in general regarding the nature of the lover and the beloved:

> First of all, love is a joint experience between two persons—but the fact that it is a joint experience does not mean that it is a similar experience to the two people involved. There are the lover and the beloved, but these two come from different countries. Often the beloved is only a stimulus for all the stored-up love which has lain quiet within the lover for a long time hitherto. And somehow every lover knows this. He feels in his soul that his love is a solitary thing. He comes to know a new,

> strange loneliness and it is this knowledge which makes him suffer. So there is only one thing for the lover to do. He must house his love within himself as best he can; he must create for himself a whole new inward world—a world intense and strange, complete in himself (18–19).

McCullers's balladeer makes it clear that the lover can be "any human creature on this earth," and that "the most outlandish people can be the stimulus for love":

> A most mediocre person can be the object of a love which is wild, extravagant, and beautiful as the poison lilies of the swamp. A good man may be the stimulus for a love both violent and debased, or a jabbering madman may bring about in the soul of someone a tender and simple idyll. Therefore, the value and quality of any love is determined solely by the lover himself. It is for this reason that most of us would rather love than be loved. Almost everyone wants to be the lover. And the curt truth is that, in a deep secret way, the state of being beloved is intolerable to many. The beloved fears and hates the lover, and with the best of reasons. For the lover is forever trying to strip bare his beloved. The lover craves any possible relation with the beloved, even if this experience can cause him only pain (19).

When *The Ballad of the Sad Café* first appeared in *Harper's Bazaar*, McCullers sent a copy of the magazine to a young army private she had recently met, Robert Walden, and in the margin beside her treatise on the failure of *eros*, she scribbled in pencil: "This is true, Bob, only when you are *not* in love."[13] Later, McCullers insisted in her essay "The Flowering Dream: Notes on Writing" that the "passionate, individual love—the old Tristan-Isolde love, the Eros love—is inferior to the love of God, to fellowship, to the love of Agape—the Greek god of the feast, the God of brotherly love—and of man. This is what I tried to show in *The Ballad of the Sad Café* in the strange love of Miss Amelia for the little hunchback, Cousin Lymon."[14] Whereas McCullers does reveal the eventual failure of *eros* and its destructive powers upon the trio in her tale, the characters achieve no redemption through *agape* (in the sense of communal affection), except for the temporal relief afforded by the café.

One could argue that McCullers's claim regarding her intentions in a work written fifteen years earlier when her emotions were deeply involved in the fiction is not wholly true.[15] Louise Westling has pointed out that McCullers's statement that *The Ballad of the Sad Café* "was intended to show the inferiority of passionate individual love to *agape*" by no means accounted "for the individual peculiarities of her characters and the sexual dimensions of their problems in love."[16] Just as McCullers herself had experienced abject grief upon her painful discovery of the transitory nature of love and the impossibility of a lasting relationship with her

Swiss friend, so, too, does Amelia suffer profoundly through her extraordinary love for Lymon, and for the café itself.

Six years after Lymon became ensconced in the café, Marvin Macy returns to town bent on revenge. The two men stare at one another with "the look of two criminals who recognize each other," (35), and Lymon becomes instantly transformed into a spirited lover. He performs every trick he knows to get Macy's attention, while Macy, in turn, alternately ignores and insults his suitor. The strange triangle takes its final turn when Amelia is reduced to accepting the role of the frustrated lover, and this time it is Lymon who cruelly spurns *her*, choosing instead the swaggering, revengeful husband who puts up with the hunchback merely to gain an ally against his wife. Lymon flirts shamelessly with Macy, apes and insults the grieving Amelia to her face, and invites her husband to move in with them. Amelia does not rebel, knowing that if she drives her rival away, Lymon will follow. The thought of being alone again, having abandoned the last vestige of her strident independence to the dwarf, is intolerable. The narrator intercedes at this point to declare that "it is better to take in your mortal enemy than face the terror of living alone" (45). Amelia's futile efforts to regain Lymon's favor parallel Macy's former attempts to woo her. Until he courted Amelia and was mysteriously transfigured by love, Macy's meanness was legendary throughout the region.

A bitter confrontation between Amelia and Macy is inevitable, an event that McCullers describes in mock-heroic fashion. The couple square off one evening in the center of the café before all the townspeople, who have watched the trio fearfully since the day Macy arrived. It is the dead of winter after an extraordinary snow, and there have been countless strange interruptions to nature's rhythms that the townspeople attribute to Macy. Along with other ominous signs a few hours before the fight begins, "a hawk with a bloody breast" flies over the town and circles "twice around the property of Miss Amelia" (47). Thirty minutes after the fight commences, Amelia's advantage is unmistakable. She pins Macy to the floor and straddles him, her strong, big hands at his throat, but the hunchback intervenes. From the counter twelve feet away where he has perched to watch the fight, Lymon sails through the air "as though he had grown hawk wings," lands upon Amelia's back, and claws furiously at her neck. When the townsfolk come to their senses, Amelia lies motionless on the floor. The narrator explains that "this was not a fight to hash over and talk about afterward; people went home and pulled the covers up over their heads" (51).

Amelia's pathetic defeat echoes the scene at the close of *Reflections in a Golden Eye,* but Amelia is not afforded the release of death. Trapped in the abyss of loneliness and isolation, she sobs fitfully "with the last of her grating, winded breath," her head in the crook of her arm. The destruction of her café and still, the theft of her worldly possessions, the sausage and grits laced with poison left behind—all mean nothing compared to the physical and spiritual decay that sets in irrevocably with the hunchback's sweeping leap. A victim of complete abandonment, the pathetic woman sits every night for three years on the front steps of her sagging house and gazes forlornly down the road upon which Lymon had first appeared. At last, in an admission of defeat, Amelia lets her hair grow ragged, and day by day her gray eyes become more crossed, "as though they sought each other out to exchange a little glance of grief and lonely recognition" (52). Finally, she hires a carpenter to board up the premises of the café, and there is, as a result, no good liquor to be had anywhere. It is rumored that those who drink from the still eight miles away will "grow warts on their livers the size of goobers" and "dream themselves into a dangerous inward world" (53). The rest of the townsfolk, in their boredom, have little to do except "walk around the millpond, stand kicking at a rotten stump, figure out what [one] can do with the old wagon wheel by the side of the road near the church," and as a last resort, "go down to the Forks Falls highway and listen to the chain gang." (53). But Amelia allows herself no such relief. She does not go to the highway like the others to seek solace in the voices of the chain gang. Yet McCullers's coda, "The Twelve Mortal Men," stands as a paean to survival and a moving illustration of the power of brotherhood, even when the union is brought on by chains of bondage.

For a recording made in 1958—seventeen years after writing *The Ballad of the Sad Café*—McCullers read the final passage of the novel, the coda of the chain gang. Although her spirits were low and her health wretched, McCullers's voice was steady and strong until she reached the final line. "Just twelve mortal men who are together," wept McCullers, her breaking voice a vital part of the recording. In her canon, the word *just* had a special connotation that heightened its irony. "*Just* is too small a word for pity," explained Mollie Lovejoy, a character she had created some fifteen years after *The Ballad of the Sad Café*. "It's like saying *just* food, *just* God."[17]

The Ballad of the Sad Café provoked no serious attention from reviewers until its appearance in the 1951 omnibus edition. In a front-page review in the Sunday *New York Herald Tribune,* Coleman Rosenberger declared the title story "condensed and brilliant writing, which carries the reader along so easily on the waves of the story that he may not at first be aware how completely he has been saturated with symbolism."[18] William P. Clancey, reviewing for *Commonweal,* called McCullers's work "metaphysical" and spoke admiringly of the "metaphysical fusion of horror and compassion" by the author whose "young American talent" was of the "very first order."[19] Robert Kee informed readers of the British *Spectator* that McCullers's style had an "Olympian dispassionateness which is designed to strengthen the violence of the human emotions with which she is often concerned. It is the same sort of effect which Hardy achieved for his characters in far more clumsily contrived sentences."[20] V. S. Pritchett insisted that McCullers was the "most remarkable novelist to come out of America for a generation" and declared that her compassion gives her characters "a Homeric moment in a universal tragedy."[21]

In his notable argument, "The Myth of the Sad Café," Albert J. Griffith contrasted McCullers's impressive mythic imagination with that of such moderns as James Joyce, T. S. Eliot, William Faulkner, Eudora Welty, and John Updike, stressing that her fellow writers had created contemporary parallels to various well-known myths, whereas McCullers shaped "her own new myth out of primitive elements."[22]

A strong body of feminist criticism of *The Ballad of the Sad Café,* as well as of McCullers's other works, emerged in the mid-1970s. Panthea Reid Broughton provided the first significant feminist reading, which viewed the tale as a fable that "shows us that rejecting those characters labeled as exclusively feminine bounces back on the rejecter and renders men and women alike incapable of love."[23] Charlene Clark's study of "male-female pairs" in both *The Ballad of the Sad Café* and *The Member of the Wedding* demonstrates effectively how McCullers's aggressive females dominate the passive males with whom they are paired and that these women vent their aggression through violence as a means of dominating the men.[24] Another notable feminist reading is Claire Kahane's "Gothic Mirrors and Feminine Identity," which treats *The Ballad of the Sad Café* as a "redefined modern Gothic fiction" and places McCullers closer to Flannery O'Connor than to any of her other contemporaries.[25] Both Robert S. Phillips and Louise Westling have addressed Isak Dinesen's considerable influence through her tale "The Monkey" upon *The Ballad of the Sad Café*.[26] Westling perceives a significant difference between the work of the two writers, noting McCullers's attempt to deny the feminine entirely and to allow a woman to function successfully as a man.

The Ballad of the Sad Café has continued to stand up well under the scrutiny of critics. Many contend that, all things considered, it is still her best work.

Notes

1. Carson McCullers, "The Ballad of the Sad Café," *Harper's Bazaar* (Aug. 1943): 72–75, 140–161; published first in book form as *"The Ballad of the Sad Café": The Novels and Stories of Carson McCullers* (Boston: Houghton Mifflin, 1951). Page references within the text are to a later edition, *"The Ballad of the Sad Café" and Collected Short Stories* (Boston: Houghton Mifflin, 1955).

2. McCullers, "The Flowering Dream: Notes on Writing" in *The Mortgaged Heart* (Boston: Houghton Mifflin, 1971), 274–275.

3. Carson McCullers to Robert Linscott, undated letter; from Robert Newton Linscott Collection, Washington University Libraries, St. Louis, Mo.

4. Katherine Anne Porter to Virginia Spencer Carr, interview, College Park, Maryland, 1 Aug. 1971; see also, Carr, *The Lonely Hunter: A Biography of Carson McCullers* (Garden City: Doubleday, 1975), 154–158.

5. *Vogue* 97 (1 Mar. 1941): 62–63, 138.

6. Mary A. Gervin, "McCullers's Frames of Reference in *The Ballad of the Sad Café*," *Pembroke Magazine* 20 (1988): 37–42.

7. McCullers, "The Twisted Trinity," *Decision* 2 (Nov.-Dec. 1941): 30; "The Twisted Trinity" (Philadelphia: Elkan-Vogel, 1946). Poem set to music by David Diamond (sheet music for piano).

8. Margaret Walsh, "Carson McCullers' Anti-Fairy Tale: 'The Ballad of the Sad Café,'" *Pembroke Magazine* 20 (1988): 43–48. Walsh writes convincingly of Lymon as a "faithfully-sketched fairy-tale dwarf" in all characteristics except his lack of a beard.

9. Robert M. Rechnitz, "The Failure of Love: The Grotesque in Two Novels by Carson McCullers," *Georgia Review* 22 (Winter 1968): 454–463. Longtime friends of McCullers have stressed that throughout her life she was naïve, honest, and childlike—rather than "childish"—qualities that they saw repeatedly in her fiction through her point-of-view characters.

10. Dawson F. Gaillard, "The Presence of the Narrator in Carson McCullers's *Ballad of the Sad Café*," *Mississippi Quarterly* 25 (Fall 1972): 419–428.

11. John McNally, "The Introspective Narrator in 'The Ballad of the Sad Café,'" *South Atlantic Bulletin* 38 (Nov. 1973): 40–44.

12. Joseph R. Millichap, "Carson McCullers's Literary Ballad," *Georgia Review* 27 (Fall 1973): 334–335.

13. Robert Walden to Carr, interview, Charlotte, N.C., 11 May 1971; from the personal archives of Robert Walden, Charlotte, N.C.

14. "The Flowering Dream," 281.

15. See Margaret B. McDowell's *Carson McCullers* (Boston: Twayne, 1980) 71–72, for an insightful discussion of the *eros/agape* theme. Important, too, is Louise Westling's "Carson McCullers' Amazon Nightmare," *Modern Fiction Studies* 28 (Autumn 1982): 465–473.

16. Louise Westling, *Sacred Groves and Ravaged Gardens: The Fiction of Eudora Welty, Carson McCullers, and Flannery O'Connor* (Athens: University of Georgia Press, 1985), 127. See also Westling's entire chapter in this book entitled "Tomboys and Revolting Femininity" (110–132) for an excellent discussion of the hermaphroditic and androgynous aspects of Miss Amelia in *The Ballad of the Sad Café.*

17. McCullers, *The Square Root of Wonderful* (Dunwoody, Ga.: Norman S. Berg, 1958), act 2, p. 99.

18. Coleman Rosenberger, "A Carson McCullers Omnibus," *New York Herald Tribune Books,* (10 June 1951): 1.

19. William P. Clancey, Review of *The Ballad of the Sad Café, Commonweal* 54 (15 June 1951): 243.

20. Robert Kee, Review of *The Ballad of the Sad Café, Spectator* 189 (12 Sept. 1952): 34.

21. V. S. Pritchett, "Books in General," *The New Statesman and Nation* 44 (2 Aug. 1952): 137–138.

22. Albert J. Griffith, "Carson McCullers's Myth of the Sad Café," *Georgia Review* 21 (Spring 1967): 46–56.

23. Panthea Reid Broughton, "Rejection of the Feminine in Carson McCullers's *The Ballad of the Sad Café,*" *Twentieth Century Literature* 20 (Jan. 1974): 34–43.

24. Charlene Clark, "Male-Female Pairs in Carson McCullers's *The Ballad of the Sad Café* and *The Member of the Wedding,*" *Notes on Contemporary Literature* 11 (Sept. 1979): 11–12.

25. Claire Kahane, "Gothic Mirrors and Feminine Identity," *Centennial Review* 24 (1980): 43–63.

26. Robert S. Phillips, "Dinesen's 'Monkey' and McCullers' 'Ballad': A Study in Literary Affinity," *Studies in Short Fiction* 1 (Spring 1964): 184–190; Louise Westling, "Carson McCullers' Amazon Nightmare," *Modern Fiction Studies* 28 (Autumn 1982): 465–473.

CHAPTER FIVE

The Member of the Wedding

Carson McCullers worked fitfully for over five years on her next novel, *The Member of the Wedding* (1946), interrupting progress on it many times to cope with the demands of life itself. Her debilitating illnesses, passions, bereavements, divorce, remarriage, the war itself—all impeded the evolution of the novel, yet also became a part of it. Whereas *Reflections in a Golden Eye* and *The Ballad of the Sad Café* seemed almost to write themselves, *The Heart Is a Lonely Hunter* and *The Member of the Wedding* gave their creator a much harder time both in conception and delivery. *The Member of the Wedding* was dedicated to Elizabeth Ames, director of Yaddo Artists Colony, who had read and offered suggestions for each of the six drafts of the novel written primarily at Yaddo during the author's several stays there.

Just as McCullers had great difficulty in settling upon the design and focus of her first novel, so, too, did she anguish for many months over the direction of what she initially called "The Bride and Her Brother."

Finally, the elusive element came to her abruptly as she chased after a fire engine in her neighborhood in Brooklyn Heights, New York, in the fall of 1940. Estranged from her husband and living temporarily in the old brownstone at 7 Middagh Street, she had been sitting over coffee and brandy with Gypsy Rose Lee when they heard the sirens and ran several blocks in pursuit. Suddenly, McCullers caught her friend by the arm and shouted: "Stop! I have it! Frankie is in love with her brother and the bride, and wants to become a member of the wedding!" McCullers trembled during their silent walk back to the house, at last certain of the shaping event in her novel, yet frightened in a sense, too, by its extraordinary revelation and her new responsibility for bringing it off.[1]

Frankie Addams was not McCullers's mirror image as an adolescent, but she was close kin in every important aspect of character and being. She and Mick, the youthful protagonist in *The Heart Is a Lonely Hunter*, evolved with much in common, having come from the same environment and social class as McCullers herself. Both are daughters of tired, wan jewelers who had hoped for far more satisfaction in their lives and careers than they actually have. The only maternal nurturing each girl receives is from the black servant (and surrogate mother) in her household. Mick has Portia Copeland and Frankie has the one-eyed Berenice Sadie Brown. Mick's mother is too busy operating her boardinghouse to be concerned with the emotional rearing of her daughter, and Frankie's mother has died in childbirth. In their restless approach to puberty, both girls fend largely for themselves. The unnamed fictional towns in which Mick and Frankie live are not unlike McCullers's own hometown as she knew it in the late 1930s. Frankie's peregrinations carry her up and down the four blocks of Front Avenue, the actual name for the street that runs parallel to McCullers's own main street, Broadway, in Columbus, Georgia. Frankie's town, too, has an army post like Fort Benning tucked into its lower pocket.

McCullers employed the same straightforward, omniscient narrative voice in *The Member of the Wedding* that had served her well in *The Heart Is a Lonely Hunter* and *Reflections in a Golden Eye*. But the voice here is more singular, personal, and poignant. *The Member of the Wedding* is Frankie's story—she *is* the member—and every significant event in the novel relates to her. This novel is also the most compressed in time of all of McCullers's long works, including her next, and final, novel, *Clock Without Hands* (1961).

The three-part structure of *The Member of the Wedding* is much like the structure of *The Heart Is a Lonely Hunter*, and in each novel there is one main event: the suicide of John Singer and the wedding of Frankie's brother. Like McCullers's first novel, *The Member of the Wedding* was planned according to a precise and harmonious design enriched by the contrapuntal fugue-like voices of the main characters.[2] In part 1, Frankie suddenly realizes who she is and where she is going. She is in love with the bride and her brother and plans to accompany them on their honeymoon, wherever it may be. Part 2 takes place the day before the wedding as the exuberant Frankie makes her plans to leave; she bids farewell to her town as though it has been poised to hear from her in her new identity as "F. Jasmine Addams." Frankie had made up the name *Jasmine* to strengthen the bond (alliteratively) with her brother and his bride, Jarvis and Janice. Part 3, strikingly like its counterpart in *The Heart Is a Lonely Hunter* both in length and importance to the action that precedes it, is a brief coda that reports the events after the wedding when Frankie painfully discovers the reality of the situation and is dragged from the honeymoon car.

In *The Heart Is a Lonely Hunter*, each character realizes upon the death of John Singer that if he is to survive he must be his own person and not the reflection of what he thinks he had seen in the deaf mute. More resilient than Mick, Frankie shores up her fragments and finds solace in a new friendship with someone her age. Frankie still has her illusions, but she accepts herself, no longer wishes to be a member of the opposite sex, and begins to go by her real name, *Frances*.

When the story opens, Frankie looks like a boy. Her hair is short, she is barefoot, and she is dressed in a pair of blue track shorts and a B.V.D. undershirt. On the edge of puberty, she yearns for a connection that will get her out of the kitchen and away from the house, where her only companions are her six-year-old cousin, John Henry West, and Berenice Sadie Brown, the housekeeper and cook who entertains Frankie and her cousin as best she can. Frankie vaguely admires her father, but finds him too preoccupied with his watch repair and jeweler's business to supervise or nurture her in any meaningful way. When she tells him (in part 2) that she will not come home after the wedding, he does not listen, but querulously demands to know what has happened to his monkey wrench and screw driver.

Throughout the novel, Frankie is caught between the injunctions of those in authority in her life, who demand that she exercise common sense and reason, and her own desperate need to fantasize about a connection with something larger than herself. Despite Royal Addams's gruff nature and apparent insensitivity to his daughter's needs, McCullers treats him sympathetically. Addams is, in fact, as close a rendering of her own father as the author dared put on paper. Frankie notes that her father "walked the dawn-stale kitchen like a person who has lost something, but has forgotten what it is that he has lost. Watching him, the old grudge was forgotten, and she felt sorry."[3]

Berenice cannot relieve the child's ambivalent and unfulfilled yearnings, although she is a nurturing and healthy influence on Frankie. Berenice instructs Frankie in motherly fashion, but her stoic acceptance of her own "caught condition" in a white man's world makes it impossible for her to understand thoroughly the child's troubled nature and her schemes to effect some kind of meaningful change in her life. As if speaking for all of her fictional brethren who inhabit the landscape of McCullers's novels and short stories, Berenice says, "We all of us somehow caught. We born this way or that way and we don't know why" (98). She makes it clear to Frankie that her skin color adds another dimension to the problems that must be faced in life: "But they done drawn completely extra bounds around all colored people. They done squeezed us off in one corner by ourself" (98).

John Henry—a spectator to most of the events—is reminiscent of Mick Kelly in his penchant for queer, childish drawings with which he has covered Frankie's kitchen walls as high as he can reach. The shabby kitchen with its strange decorations has the look of a "crazy house," and Frankie is vaguely afraid. "The world is certainly a sudden place" (6), she announces to Berenice and John Henry, having just learned that Jarvis is getting married to a girl from Winter Hill, Georgia. His coming from Alaska, where he was stationed in the army, and marrying a girl from a small town in his home state is a curious coincidence, thinks Frankie, whose mind leaps to thoughts of Eskimos, snow, frozen seas, and polar bears. The fact that John Henry has seen snow gives him a special status that she herself woefully lacks, a status that makes his presence more acceptable to her. Frankie often joins

John Henry and Berenice at the kitchen table for three-handed bridge, and in their boredom they sometimes lay down their cards and begin to "criticize the Creator" and tell each other how, if they were God, they would improve the world.

Just as the soul rots with boredom in Amelia's mill town in *The Ballad of the Sad Café*, so, too, does Frankie's during the "dog days" of summer in her microcosmic world of the kitchen. Because her country is at war (the action of the novel is compressed into four months during the first year or two of World War II), Frankie wants to be a Marine and win gold medals for bravery (her inability to actually "join the war" intensifies her restlessness and makes her even more irrational). She fantasizes giving a quart of blood a week—still another means of attaining kinship—so that it "would be in the veins of Australians and Fighting French and Chinese, all over the whole world" (20).

While McCullers was writing this part of *The Member of the Wedding*, New York City was experiencing a wartime blackout, and she imagined women being conscripted to military service and herself going overseas as a soldier or a foreign correspondent. In the spring of 1943, she wrote friends that she had "gone to the top" in trying to get hired as an overseas reporter, but those who knew of her efforts did not take them seriously.[4] She spoke, too, of adopting a war orphan, but that effort—or "whim," as some called it—did not materialize, either. Similarly, Frankie is "rejected" by the war, the blood bank, and her father as well, who asks: "Who is this great big long-legged twelve-year-old blunderbuss who still wants to sleep with her old Papa?" (20). In retaliation for this rejection and other imagined slights, Frankie tells Berenice that she would like to "tear down" the whole town.

In an essay entitled "Love's Not Time's Fool," published in *Mademoiselle* in 1943, McCullers took the stance of a war wife, having recently received what she described as a "noble conciliatory letter" from Reeves McCullers in which he declared that he still loved her and was over his "strange sickness" that had made him do the "ignoble things" that led to their estrangement.[5] After their divorce, he had gone back into the army, was now a second lieutenant, and would soon be going overseas, Reeves wrote her. McCullers, too, was of a different heart. Annemarie Clarac-Schwarzenbach had died in a bicycle accident in Switzerland over a year earlier, and McCullers was receptive to a "new Reeves," she declared.[6]

In her personal life as in her fiction, McCullers tried relentlessly to drive away her demons and to commit herself to something beyond her own separate being. Just as Mick wanted to be a member of a "bunch," so, too, does Frankie, but she fears that the only group into which she can fit is the troupe of freaks at the midway of the county fair. She had stood with John Henry in front of the booth of the "Half-Man Half-Woman" and imagined that all of the freaks were watching her in a "secret way" and trying to connect their eyes with hers as though to say "we know you" (17). Frankie is drawn, too, to the jail, where she feels the eyes of the convicts upon her as she walks back and forth in front of the barred windows. "Do you think I will grow into a Freak?" she asks Berenice. "Certainly not, I trust Jesus," replies Berenice (18). But Frankie does not have Berenice's faith. Again and again, Frankie asks herself where she could possibly go to become the kind of person she envisions herself.

In focusing on the issues that lie at the heart of Frankie's identity crisis, the narrator discusses her aloneness in light of the companionship that everyone else seems to have in his or her life:

> She was an I person who had to walk around and do things by herself. All other people had a *we* to claim, all others except her. When Berenice said *we,* she meant Honey and Big Mama, her lodge, or her church. The *we* of her father was the store. All members of clubs have a *we* to belong to and to talk about. The soldiers in the army can say *we,* and even the criminals on chaingangs. But the old Frankie had had no *we* to claim, unless it would be the terrible summer *we* of her and John Henry and Berenice—and that was the last *we* in the world she wanted (35).

Suddenly, Frankie has an epiphany, an illumination not unlike McCullers's own as she chased after the fire engine with Gypsy Rose Lee. Frankie decides that her brother and his bride are her *"we of me,"* a realization that causes her "squeezed heart" to suddenly open and divide. She tells John Henry that she is going off with them after the wedding and "to whatever place that they will ever go. . . . It's like I've known it all my life, that I belong to be with them. I love the two of them so much" (38).

On the day before the wedding as Frankie, Berenice, and John Henry sit and talk in the kitchen, Frankie is distracted by the tuning of the piano in the next room. The tuner plays repeatedly the scale "up until the seventh note," then hesitates there, unable to finish. Frankie thinks it strange that the "G" and "A" notes are so markedly different since they are "side by side there on the piano just as close together as the other notes" (89), and her thoughts of separateness return. "Doesn't it strike you as strange that I am I, and you are you?" she demands of Berenice. "I am F. Jasmine Addams. And you are Berenice Sadie Brown. And we can look at each other, and touch each other, and stay together year in and year out in the same room. Yet always I am I, and you are you. And I can't ever be anything else but me, and you can't ever be anything else but you" (94).

Frankie tells Berenice that she wants to know everybody in the whole world, and that going off with Janice and Jarvis after the wedding will make it happen. Her obsession to be joined in a "we of me" with her brother and his bride is extended now to include the whole human race, and she is determined to become the sum of all she imagines. Her dream is destined to fail, of course, as surely as the soft August moths are caught in their "irony of fate," as Frankie refers to their plight, when, attracted by the light, they press against the window screen and die (12). At the wedding she discovers what she has secretly feared: that certain things will always be beyond her power. When her father ejects her, screaming, from the honeymoon car, Frankie is forced to admit defeat. Afterwards, she sits with Berenice in the back of the bus as they return home from Winter Hill. Overcome by self-hatred after taking momentary solace in thinking of the "mean word" she had never used before ("*nigger*"), she wants the "whole world to die" (118).

Frankie has been haunted during the course of her summer by several actual deaths of people in her town. One was the murder of a young black boy who was found dead behind her father's store, his slashed throat open "like a crazy shivering mouth that spoke ghost words into the April sun" (76). McCullers's image foreshadows Frankie's own situation later, when she stands tongue-tied in the bride's room just before the wedding, yearning to say "I love the two of you so much and you are the we of me. Please take me with you from the wedding, for we belong to be together" (119), but she can utter not a word. The death of an uncle that summer had made her even more aware of her mortality, and in thinking of him, she remembers those she has known who have died who "feel nothing, hear nothing, see nothing: only black," and she is struck by the "terrible finality of it all" (77). Although she had declared earlier that she would shoot herself in the head with her father's pistol if the bride and her brother did not take her with them, she cannot pull the trigger because "deadness was blackness, nothing but pure terrible blackness that went on and on and never ended until the end of all the world" (125). Frankie is further shocked by the death of John Henry, who screams in pain for three days before dying of spinal meningitis.

Frankie's preoccupation with death was doubtless influenced by the deaths of three people in McCullers's own life while she was working on the novel. One of the children in her neighborhood, a little boy, died of spinal meningitis, and another, five-year-old Robin Mullin, who lived next door, drowned. Robin came often to the Smith family's kitchen for treats and lingered, much as John Henry did, feeling free to come and go because the same servant kept house and cooked for both households. Like John Henry, the child considered himself a "member of the kitchen."[7] The death that affected McCullers the most profoundly, however, was that of her father, whose body was found in his jewelry store on August 1, 1944. Although the newspapers reported it a heart attack, intimates of the family claimed that the melancholy jeweler had, in fact, shot himself.[8]

The night that Frankie returns from the wedding, bitter and angry, she writes her father a farewell letter in which she explains that she can stand her existence no longer. She takes the pistol from her father's bureau drawer and heads for the train station with a vague idea of jumping on any freight car that happened to come along, but the station is closed and there are no trains expected until morning. After walking the "night-empty streets" until she ends up in the alley where the youth was found that spring with his throat slashed, she decides to wait for the train at the bar of the Blue Moon, the hotel in which she had kept a "date" with a soldier and naïvely ended up in his room (she had cracked him over the head with a water pitcher to ward off his advances and told no one of her misadventure). When a policeman discovers her at the Blue Moon—her father having "sicked the Law on her"—and asks where she "was headed," Frankie pictures an enormous canyon between herself and all the places she has formerly envisioned. She recognizes that her "plans for the movies or the Marines were only child plans that would never work" and tries to think of the "littlest, ugliest place she knew, for to run away there could not be considered so very wrong. 'Flowering Branch,' " she replies (128).

In the novel's final scene, it is November and John Henry is dead. Frankie goes by "Frances" now and remembers her little cousin only as he used to be. The old familiar kitchen has been renovated, the house has been sold, and Frankie and her father are moving to a home in the suburbs that they will share with John Henry's parents. Berenice, too, is in the process of making changes. She has given "quit notice" to the Addams family and plans to marry again.

Frankie has not spoken once of her brother's wedding since that fateful day and devotes her time now to poetry, radar, school, and her new friend, Mary Littlejohn, who was once the "pasty-faced girl with pigtails" chosen instead of Frankie for club membership by the older girls in the neighborhood. She tells Berenice as they prepare to leave the kitchen for good that she and Mary are planning "to travel around the world together."

As she gazes out the window, awaiting the arrival of her friend, Frankie notices that the "last pale colors" of the day appear "crushed and cold on the horizon. Dark, when it came, would come on quickly, as it does in wintertime," interjects the narrator (132).

"I am simply mad about—" but Frances leaves the sentence unfinished, for "with an instant shock of happiness," she hears the "ringing of the bell" (132).

Desperate to escape the "caught condition" of which Berenice has spoken, Frankie allows the "shock of happiness" to divert her attention from that which she is "mad about." However, given the deterministic theme that runs evenly through this and other works by McCullers, there is no reason to believe that Frankie's new-found contentment will be anything but short-lived.

Early reviews of *The Member of the Wedding* were, for the most part, laudatory. George Dangerfield recommended the book to readers of *The Saturday Review of Literature* as a "marvelous piece of writing" and called the author "unique." Although "nothing occurs here," he wrote, every page is "filled with a sense of something having happened, happening, and about to happen. This is in itself a considerable technical feat; and, beyond that, there is magic in it."[9] Isa Kapp compared McCullers to Thomas Wolfe and informed readers of the *New York Times Book Review* that McCullers's language had the "freshness, quaintness and gentleness of a sensitive child."[10] Rarely had "emotional turbulence been so delicately conveyed," he added. Marguerite Young, writing for *The Kenyon Review*, called McCullers a "poetic symbolist, a seeker after those luminous meanings which always do transcend the boundaries of the stereotyped, the conventional, and the so-called normal."[11]

Notes

1. Virginia Spencer Carr, *The Lonely Hunter: A Biography of Carson McCullers* (Garden City: Doubleday, 1975), 121.

2. Carson McCullers, "The Vision Shared," *Theatre Arts* 34 (Apr. 1950): 30; reprinted in *The Mortgaged Heart*, 265.

3. McCullers, *The Member of the Wedding* (Boston: Houghton Mifflin, 1946), 44. All page references within the text are to this edition.

4. Carr, *The Lonely Hunter*, 227–228.

5. "Love's Not Time's Fool" (signed by "A War Wife"), *Mademoiselle*, 16 (Apr. 1943): 95.

6. Carr, 232.

7. Lamar Smith to Carr, interview, Perry, Fla., 3 Oct. 1970.

8. David Diamond and Vannie Copland Jackson to Carr, conversation, Columbus, Ga., 23 Oct. 1987. At the close of a symposium held at Columbus College in Columbus, Ga., to commemorate the twentieth anniversary of McCullers's death, intimates of McCullers (who had known her in her hometown or in New York) spoke freely about the alleged heart attack and said that Lamar Smith's death was "definitely a suicide."

9. George Dangerfield, "An Adolescent's Four Days," *The Saturday Review of Literature* (30 Mar. 1946): 15.

10. Isa Kapp, "One Summer: Three Lives," *New York Times Book Review* (24 Mar. 1946): 5.

11. Marguerite Young, "Metaphysical Fiction," *The Kenyon Review*, 9 (Winter 1947): 151–155.

CHAPTER SIX

The Plays: *The Member of the Wedding* and *The Square Root of Wonderful*

Less than four years after the publication of *The Member of the Wedding*, McCullers—still seeking after those illusory but "luminous meanings"—had transformed her novel into a play and was sitting in her producer's living room on the opening night of its Broadway debut. Even though she was too ill to attend the premiere, McCullers was exuberant as she awaited visits from cast members and the laudatory reviews that followed the first performance of the theatrical triumph that profoundly affected the direction of her life.

It is unlikely that McCullers would have attempted to write for the theater had it not been for the encouragement of Tennessee Williams. Yet the realization of *The Member of the Wedding* as a tremendously successful play on Broadway is attributed largely to McCullers's own inspired writing, her sheer will, and her indomitable courage—courage that, despite extraordinary personal adversity, sustained her during the three years immediately preceding the play's opening.

McCullers's career as a playwright actually began when she was a child. In "How I Began to Write," published in *Mademoiselle* before her acclaim in the theater, McCullers told of her involvement as a child in all phases of play production as writer, director, and technician.[1] The front sitting room of her parents' home served as an auditorium for the family and neighbors, while the back sitting room functioned as a stage. Heavy sliding wooden doors served handily as a curtain between the two rooms. McCullers described her repertory—in which she and her two siblings played all the roles—as "eclectic, running from hashed-over movies to Shakespeare and shows" that she made up and sometimes wrote down in her "nickel Big Chief notebooks."[2] At fifteen she discovered Eugene O'Neill and wrote a "three-acter about revenge and incest—the curtain rose on a graveyard and, after scenes of assorted misery, fell on a catafalque." She said that her first serious creative endeavor was a play called "The Faucet," set in New Zealand. Next, under the influence of Nietzsche, whom she had just discovered, she wrote "The Fire of Life," a play in rhymed verse that featured two characters, Nietzsche and Jesus Christ. These were reading plays that did not lend themselves to the stage presentations typical of her juvenile acting troupe, she explained. Her third major literary effort was "A Reed of

Pan," a novel that had as its protagonist a musician seduced by jazz.[3] Having tried her hand at a novel, McCullers abandoned her bent for playwriting and might never have attempted it again had it not been for a letter some fifteen years later from Tennessee Williams and an invitation to spend a few days with him on Nantucket during the summer of 1946.

When the playwright wrote to her, they had never met. Williams had not even heard of McCullers or her work until May of that year when he read *The Member of the Wedding* and was so moved by it that he sent her a fan letter, the first such letter the playwright had written in his life.[4] *The Glass Menagerie*—then in its second year on Broadway—had brought Williams extraordinary acclaim and won for him the New York Drama Critics' Circle Award. The playwright was having difficulty completing a new long play (*Summer and Smoke*), and he hoped that a change of scenery to some quiet ocean retreat would help. Before leaving New York City, Williams met Jordan Massee, Carson McCullers's cousin from Macon, Georgia, and told Massee that he had just written McCullers an admiring letter. Struck by the remarkable compassion inherent in *The Member of the Wedding*, Williams had sat up all night to finish reading it. "When I read *The Member of the Wedding*, I thought that she was possibly the greatest novelist then alive in America and told her so," said Williams.[5]

Flattered by the playwright's strange invitation and pleased to be sought out by a literary artist of such note, McCullers readily accepted. She had not seen *The Glass Menagerie*—she had seen, in fact, only two or three professionally produced plays in her life—but practically overnight she took the ferry to Nantucket and by the first week of June was ensconced in an old gray-frame cottage at 31 Pine Street with Williams and his companion from New Orleans, Pancho Rodriguez. Buoyed now by Williams's enthusiasm and goaded, as well, by Edmund Wilson's recent scathing review of *The Member of the Wedding* in *The New Yorker,* McCullers set about to try her hand at a dramatic adaptation of her novel.[6] Wilson had found the kitchen scenes in McCullers's novel "admirably atmospheric" and the characters droll and natural, but he thought that the novel as a whole was undramatic, formless, and pointless.

"Carson was a natural writer. She knew what she wanted to do from the onset," said Williams. "If she wanted to ask me something or to read some lines aloud for my reaction, she would, but that was rare. She accepted almost no advice about how to adapt *The Member of the Wedding*. I did not suggest lines to her more than once or twice, and then she would usually have her own ideas and say, 'Tenn, honey, thank you, but I know all I need to know.' "[7]

Although Williams volunteered that summer to introduce McCullers to Audrey Wood (the agent who had launched him so successfully in the theater)—and even to take McCullers's draft of her new play to Wood for a reading—she declined on the grounds that she already had an agent, Ann Watkins, and did not think it fair to allow someone else to represent her for the dramatic form of *The Member of the Wedding*. In August 1946, having spent only a month working on the play on Nantucket with Williams, McCullers turned the manuscript over to Watkins with instructions for her to try to find a Broadway producer as soon as possible.

Scarcely a year later, having come to Paris at the end of 1946 to spend a year abroad writing as a Guggenheim fellow, McCullers suffered a second stroke. For a time she had no lateral vision in her right eye, and the right side of her face was numb. Severely impaired, too, was her mobility on her entire left side. McCullers attributed her condition to the distress that she suffered upon hearing what had happened to her dramatic adaption of *The Member of the Wedding*, Watkins having negotiated with the Theatre Guild in New York City to produce it *if* McCullers would allow an experienced playwright to collaborate with her. In what she described later as a "lapse into insanity," and by others as a "moment of weakness," McCullers agreed to the collaboration and signed a contract with Greer Johnson, whom Watkins had recommended to help revise the script (McCullers knew nothing about Greer's reputation or his work, and they had never met).[8] Upon reading her collaborator's revision, she was adamant about having nothing more to do with him or his script.

At the beginning of 1948, having suffered yet another stroke (and having been committed briefly to a psychiatric clinic in Manhattan for attempted suicide), McCullers took heart in her creative life once more and began to dictate a thorough revision of her play. She soon had a draft ready to show Audrey Wood, who agreed to handle the play since her new client had disassociated herself from both Greer and Watkins. But Wood told McCullers that the play definitely needed more work. In the meantime, McCullers had sent the revision to Williams in Rome, who read it and cabled her: "SCRIPT A THOUSAND TIMES BETTER." McCullers knew, however, that Williams would not have used the comparative *better*—regardless of the degree—if he thought the play truly acceptable and ready for production. Although she had turned a deaf ear to his suggestions when they worked together on Nantucket, McCullers replied now that she looked forward to any advice that he cared to give her.

Producer Cheryl Crawford advised McCullers about directors, casting, and lighting, but turned her down when asked if she would be interested in producing the play. Robert Whitehead—who with Oliver Rea and Stanley Martineau eventually produced *The Member of the Wedding*—recalled that Crawford told him before he agreed to the venture that McCullers ought to "throw it in an ash can."[9] When Audrey Wood approached Whitehead with the revised script in the late spring of 1949, the producer "bought it on the first submission" and, with McCullers's approval, asked Harold Clurman to direct it.[10]

By the time the play went into rehearsal, Ethel Waters and Julie Harris had been signed for the principal roles, and every part was cast except for the role of John Henry West, which was assigned, finally, to five-year-old Brandon de Wilde, who had never acted before and could not read. The child's father, Fritz de Wilde (who was cast as Jarvis Addams, the bridegroom) read the entire play aloud to him to help him learn his lines, and in the process, young Brandon learned the lines of everyone else as well, much to the chagrin of Waters, whom he prompted regularly until she told him, "Now, honey, I don't want you to bother me anymore."[11]

When McCullers first met Lester Polokov, who designed the set for *The Member of the Wedding,* she told him: "I don't know what to say to you. I don't know anything about the theater. I've only seen about six plays in my life and most of them were set on the stage of my high school back in Georgia, but I'd like to help." Polokov was amazed (and amused) by her childlike naïveté and told her not to worry. "We will work it out, Carson," he promised.[12]

On December 22, 1949, *The Member of the Wedding*—dedicated to McCullers's husband—opened at the Walnut Theatre in Philadelphia. Despite its superb cast, everyone connected with the play knew that its four hours of running time was much too long for a

Broadway audience. They met late into the night after the final curtain in an attempt to figure out how to salvage the production, with McCullers herself insisting on having the final word. It was *her* play they were getting ready to carve up, she reminded them, and after her last experience with a "script doctor" (her phrase for Greer Johnson) she had no intention of allowing anyone else to say how it was to be rewritten or cut. Williams, in Philadelphia for the opening, agreed with Clurman and Whitehead that the only thing that kept the play from "working" was the scene in the barroom (the one scene that he had helped McCullers write during her revision of the play). Clurman was convinced that the barroom scene broke the mood and was not a part of the play's organic unity. With McCullers's approval, the play opened the next night without the scene in question and ran with only minor changes during its nine-day tryout. For a week before the play's New York opening on January 5, 1950, daily articles ran in the New York papers to alert the theatergoing public to expect a new Broadway hit. From the moment the curtain opened on a full house of first-nighters at the Empire Theatre, there was no doubt that *The Member of the Wedding* would be a box office success. The audience threw programs and hats into the air and gave a standing ovation amidst boisterous cheers for Waters and Harris, "and for the little boy who almost stole the show," said Clurman.[13] Long lines formed at the box office the next day, and the house was a sellout for weeks—and then months—in advance.

Most of the play's opening night critics were similarly impressed, although some faulted the production for its structure and lack of dramatic movement. Howard Barnes complained that the play was structurally weak and lacked a sense of the dramatic, but praised the acting.[14] Brooks Atkinson insisted that the play's lack of dramatic movement "did not matter. . . . It may not be a play, but it is art," he said.[15] William Hawkins reported that he had "never before heard what happened last night at the curtain calls . . . when hundreds cried out as if with one voice for Ethel Waters and Julie Harris."[16]

Predictably, *The Member of the Wedding* swept the awards field for theater in the spring of 1950. McCullers's play received seventeen of a possible twenty-five votes by the New York drama critics for what they considered the top honors for American theater for the period from April 1, 1949, through March 31, 1950.[17] The night that the New York Drama Critics' Awards were announced, the play's backers knew that in light of past history, the prize meant immediate additional advance sales of at least $150,000.[18] On April 25, 1950, McCullers received the gold medal of the Theatre Club, Inc., for the "best play by an American author produced during the year." The fact that *The Member of the Wedding* was an adaptation kept McCullers out of the running for a Pulitzer, which went that year to the musical, *South Pacific.* However, in a *New York Times* article about the awards (entitled "Second-Hand Drama"), Brooks Atkinson pointed out that only three notable plays written directly for the stage had been produced during the current theater season, and of the three plays that won a Drama Critics' Circle Award for 1949–1950, *The Member of the Wedding* "came closest to Pulitzer prize specifications" since both playwright and setting were American.[19] On May 1, 1950, *The Member of the Wedding* won the Donaldson awards as the "best play of last season" and the "best first play by an author to be produced on Broadway." Harold Clurman received the Donaldson "best director" award for *The Member of the Wedding,* and Brandon de Wilde won for the "best supporting performance" (Ethel Waters was edged out by Shirley Booth in William Inge's *Come Back Little Sheba* as "best female performer" of the season).

The Member of the Wedding closed on March 17, 1951, after 501 performances, having grossed over $1,112,000 for its Broadway run alone. For the first time in her life, McCullers had "more pennies in her pocket than she knew how to spend," said her cousin, Jordan Massee.[20] A month after the play closed on Broadway, it was published by New Directions and selected as the April 1951 offering of the Fireside Theatre, which immeasurably boosted McCullers's profits by sending the play out to over ten thousand subscribers. *The Member of the Wedding* received still another honor in 1951 upon its selection as one of the "top ten plays of the year" for inclusion in *The Burns Mantle Best Plays of 1949–1950*, edited by drama critic John Chapman, who recounted in his introduction to the book the play's extraordinary history.[21] Chapman recounted, also, the reservations to which countless critics had clung (and he was no exception), that *The Member of the Wedding* was not *exactly* a play. Then he quoted what McCullers herself had said about the matter in an essay written for *Theatre Arts*:

> *The Member of the Wedding* is unconventional because it is not a *literal* kind of play. It is an inward play and the conflicts are inward conflicts. The antagonist is not personified, but is a human condition of life: the sense of moral isolation. In this respect *The Member of the Wedding* has an affinity with classical plays—which we are not used to in the modern theatre where the protagonist and antagonist are present in palpable conflict on the stage. The play has other abstract values; it is concerned with the weight of time, the hazard of human existence, bolts of chance. The reaction of the characters to these abstract phenomena projects the movement of the play. Some observers who failed to apprehend this modus operandi felt the play to be fragmentary because they did not account for this aesthetic concept. . . . Some observers have wondered if any drama as unconventional as this should be called a play. I cannot comment on that. I only know that

The Member of the Wedding is a vision that a number of artists have realized with fidelity and love.[22]

* * *

Carson McCullers was the author, too, of a little-known, second play, *The Square Root of Wonderful,* which opened on Broadway nearly eight years after the premiere of *The Member of the Wedding*. The reception of *this* play, however (by audiences and critics alike), was anything but enthusiastic.

McCullers conceived the piece originally as a play and worked on it sporadically from 1952 until 1956, along with her novel, *Clock Without Hands*. This four-year period was scarred by McCullers's continued ill health, the suicide of her husband, and perhaps the most devastating single event in her life, the death of her mother. Sick of heart yet salved by the will to keep writing, McCullers retained the essential features of the story line that eventually became *The Square Root of Wonderful,* but altered the characterization (and certain other features of the tale) sufficiently to cast its disparate parts into a long short story entitled "Who Has Seen the Wind?"[23] Yet she could not abandon altogether her original plan to make a play of the story and soon resurrected her several scripts.

In a preface to the published version of *The Square Root of Wonderful,* McCullers commented upon its autobiographical roots: "I recognized many of the compulsions that made me write this play. My husband wanted to be a writer and his failure in that was one of the disappointments that led to his death. When I started *The Square Root of Wonderful* my mother was very ill and after a few months she died. I wanted to re-create my mother—to remember her tranquil beauty and sense of joy in life. So, unconsciously, the life-death theme of *The Square Root of Wonderful* emerged."[24]

The play went through more than a dozen drafts, six or eight by McCullers alone and a handful of assorted other scripts written in collaboration with her several producers and directors. The play's first director was Albert Marre, who, having successfully directed *Kismet, Saint Joan, The Chalk Garden,* and a number of other plays, was invited by producer Arnold Saint Suber to direct *The Square Root of Wonderful.* Marre, along with Saint Suber, worked intensively with McCullers through six different scripts for over a year, but when Saint Suber announced that the script was ready to be cast and produced, Marre was on the West Coast and unavailable. Jose Quintero, who was selected to replace Marre, worked with McCullers and Saint Suber until the play's disastrous opening at the McCarter Theatre in Princeton on October 10, 1957, then left the play (though his name stayed on the credits for the Broadway opening).

The afternoon that Quintero resigned, McCullers called the cast together and told them: "I have never directed a play, and I have never seen anyone direct a play, but I wrote this play, and I know what the characters are and what I want them to be. Now you can go home if you want, but if you'd like to stay, I'll take over and do the best I can."[25] No one left. As though a single voice, the cast sang out: "We want you. We'll stay!"

According to Anne Baxter, who played Mollie Lovejoy, the lead role, "Carson's play—the child—was dying, and she knew it."[26] Baxter believed that the chief problem was that McCullers "simply could not rewrite." Albert Marre was convinced, however, that McCullers "*could* rewrite, but not the kind of square, so-called theatrical craftsman writing that the others tried to require of her."[27]

George Keathley, Quintero's eventual replacement, took the play from Princeton to Philadelphia for a nine-day run in an attempt to work out its problems, while the playwright herself and others assisted in major revisions. In a statement to the *Philadelphia Inquirer* just before the play's opening in Philadelphia, McCullers told a reporter that one of the main difficulties for a writer was "to handle tragedy and comedy almost simultaneously," but that the two elements had to be present "with the proper emotional progression."[28] McCullers wrote later (in her preface to the published version of *The Square Root of Wonderful*) of the emotional flexibility that a reader of novels has—with "time to reflect before he is pushed on to the next action"—in contrast to the *lack* of that kind of flexibility on the part of the theater-goer, who must respond immediately to the "absurd and painful truths of life" in a single line. "I have learned this in my work in the theater: the author must work alone until the intentions of his play are fulfilled—until the play is as finished as the author can make it. Once a play is in rehearsal, a playwright must write under unaccustomed pressure, and alas, what he had in mind is often compromised. That is why of the five or six evolutions this play went through I prefer to publish the one which follows. It is the last one I wrote before the production was set in motion and is the most nearly the truth of what I want to say in *The Square Root of Wonderful*."[29]

In the play, McCullers paints a dramatic portrait (as highly charged autobiographically as the one revealed in *The Member of the Wedding*) in which the protagonist is a woman named Mollie Lovejoy, whose alcoholic husband (Philip) is a failed writer of one successful novel. They have been married twice to each other and have been twice divorced. At the play's opening, Philip has just been released from a mental hospital. He still adores Mollie and goes to see her and their twelve-year-old son, Paris. But when he learns that Mollie has fallen in love with someone else (an architect named John Tucker), a man she hardly knows—who is already ensconced in her home—Philip commits suicide.[30] Tucker plans to build for Mollie and her son a new house (in effect, a new life) and gives evidence of becoming the reliable and nurturing father figure to her son that Philip was not.

The Square Root of Wonderful was soundly drubbed upon its opening on Broadway at the National Theatre on October 30, 1957, and it closed after forty-five performances. Whereas first-night critics commended Baxter for her brilliant performance as Mollie Lovejoy, the consensus was that the play could not survive its "stilted dialogue," "wooden action," and "unconvincing characters" (especially the young Paris Lovejoy). McCullers conceded that the child changed little during the course of the play, but defended her conceptualization of Paris in that it was primarily through him that the "proper emotional progression" of the other characters could be seen.[31] The play demonstrated that it was the adults in the tale who had to gain emotional maturity, that, in effect, it was they—not Paris—who were the children.

Reviewers agreed that comparisons of McCullers's new play with *The Member of the Wedding* were inevitable, and it seemed to those who knew McCullers personally (and of her increasingly debilitating illnesses) that writing for the theater was not her forte.[32] The production of *The Square Root of Wonderful* taught the playwright what she perceived to be a bitter lesson, and she vowed never again to attempt anything for the theater. In her preface to the published version of *The Square Root of Wonderful,* McCullers said that she found the "picayune last-minute changes" irritating, although she admitted that they were important since every weakness in the script becomes "magnified on the stage."[33]

John Leggett, who edited the hardcopy edition for Houghton Mifflin, recalled that McCullers was deeply resentful of the rewrites that had been made without her permission in the acting version of *The Square Root of Wonderful*: "In working with her, I made several suggestions for minor changes, and she nodded, saying 'Yes, that's fine, Jack. Put it in like that.' When I protested that these were *my* words, that I didn't presume to write the play for her, she said ruefully, 'Why not? Everybody else has!' "[34]

More than a curtain dropped when the play closed on December 7, 1957. McCullers had failed to work out in it the ambivalent love/hatred emotions kindled repeatedly, both in actuality and memory, by her husband and mother. Unlike *The Member of the Wedding,* which had given McCullers emotional release as well as extraordinary acclaim and financial security, *The Square Root of Wonderful* had become its opposite for the dejected playwright—"the square root of humiliation." Coping with a collaborator on *The Member of the Wedding* before producing a script that was, finally, wholly hers, and that became a prizewinning play with a long run was one thing; but to have *The Square Root of Wonderful* carved up beyond recognition by the play's producers and directors was quite another, a dejection from which McCullers never quite recovered. Tennessee Williams once told her in speaking of his own career as a playwright: "It takes a tough old bird to work in the theater."[35] "Carson *was* tough," said Williams, "like this marble-topped table," he added, pounding it for emphasis, but he knew, too, that she had no intention of submitting herself wittingly ever again to the hazards and "bolts of chance" by writing for the theater.[36]

Notes

1. Carson McCullers, "How I Began to Write," *Mademoiselle* (Sept. 1948): 191, 157–158; reprinted in *The Mortgaged Heart* (Boston: Houghton Mifflin, 1971), 249–251.
2. "How I Began to Write," in *The Mortgaged Heart*, 249.
3. "How I Began to Write," in *The Mortgaged Heart*, 249.
4. Tennessee Williams to Virginia Spencer Carr, interview, New Orleans, La. 30 Jan. 1972.
5. Williams to Carr, 30 Jan. 1972.
6. Edmund Wilson, "Two Books That Leave You Blank: Carson McCullers, Siegfried Sassoon," *New Yorker* 22 (30 Mar. 1946): 87.
7. Williams to Carr, 30 Jan. 1972.
8. Carr, *The Lonely Hunter: A Biography of Carson McCullers* (Garden City: Doubleday, 1975), 298–299.
9. Robert Whitehead to Carr, interview, New York City, 29 July 1972.

10. Audrey Wood to Carr, interview, New York City, 19 Mar. 1973.

11. Lester Polakov to Carr, interview, New York City, 20 May 1971; also, Harold Clurman to Carr, interview, New York City, 24 May 1971.

12. Polakov to Carr, 20 May 1971.

13. Clurman to Carr, 24 May 1971.

14. Howard Barnes, "*The Member of the Wedding*: A Review," *New York Herald Tribune* (6 Jan. 1950): 12.

15. Brooks Atkinson, "*The Member of the Wedding*: A Review," *New York Times* (6 Jan. 1950): 26.

16. William Hawkins, "Waters, Harris Roles Spark Wedding," *New York World-Telegram and The Sun* (6 Jan. 1950): 32.

17. J. P. Shanley, "McCullers' Drama Wins Critics Prize," *New York Times* (6 Apr. 1950): sec. L, p. 41.

18. Lewis Funke, "Ironic Note on the Critic Circle's Best American Play," *New York Times* (6 April 1950): sec. 2, p. 1. According to a *New York Times* article, *South Pacific* was ineligible for a Drama Critics' Circle Award because it opened later than the specified award period, but was eligible for the Pulitzer, which had a different cutoff period. See also Ward Morehouse, "Georgia's Carson McCullers Writes Year's Best Play," *Atlanta Journal Magazine* (30 Apr. 1950): 5.

19. See also Brooks Atkinson, "Three People: 'The Member of the Wedding' Superbly Acted by an Excellent Company," *New York Times* (15 January 1950): sec. 2, p. 1. Runner-up to *The Member of the Wedding* for a New York Drama Critics' Circle Award was William Inge's *Come Back Little Sheba* (four votes). Gian-Carlo Menotti's *The Consul* was named "best musical of the year," and T. S. Eliot's *The Cocktail Party* was voted "best foreign play."

20. Jordan Massee to Carr, interview, New York City, 17 July 1973.

21. John Chapman, ed., *Burns Mantle Best Plays of 1949–1950* (New York: Dodd, Mead, 1950).

22. "The Vision Shared," *Theatre Arts* (Apr. 1950): 30.

23. McCullers, "Who Has Seen the Wind?" *Mademoiselle* 42 (Sept. 1956): 156–157, 174–188.

24. McCullers, "A Personal Preface," *The Square Root of Wonderful* (Dunwoody, Ga.: Norman S. Berg, 1971) vii–x.

25. Massee to Carr, 24 July 1971.

26. Anne Baxter to Carr, interview, New York City, 1 Mar. 1972.

27. Albert Marre to Carr, telephone interview, New York City, 4 May 1973.

28. "Playwright Tells of Pangs," *Philadelphia Inquirer* (13 Oct. 1957): sec. B pp. 1, 5.

29. McCullers, "A Personal Preface," *The Square Root of Wonderful*, ix.

30. McCullers and her former music teacher, Mary Tucker, were reconciled in 1951 and attended together the play version of *The Member of the Wedding*, a work that McCullers acknowledged could never have been written had it not been for her love of Mrs. Tucker and their subsequent estrangement. McCullers's use of the name *Tucker* for the architect whom Mollie Lovejoy planned to marry, and the name *Lovejoy* itself expressed for her the *love* and *joy* she felt in having regained the love and friendship of Mary Tucker that she feared she had lost forever. After their reconciliation, McCullers visited Mrs. Tucker and her family in Virginia, and they continued to see each other once or twice a year until McCullers's death in 1967.

31. "Playwright Tells of Pangs," *Philadelphia Inquirer* (13 Oct. 1957): sec. B pp. 1, 5.

32. Arnold Saint Suber to Carr, telephone interview, 17 Dec. 1970; also, Jose Quintero to Carr, interview, Columbus, Ga., 11 Feb. 1972; and Anne Baxter to Carr, interview, New York City, 1 Mar. 1972.

33. McCullers, "A Personal Preface," *The Square Root of Wonderful*, ix.

34. John Leggett to Carr, letter, 3 Apr. 1972.

35. Williams to Carr, 30 Jan. 1972.

36. Williams to Carr, 30 Jan. 1972.

CHAPTER SEVEN

Clock Without Hands

"Darling, I have lost my soul," Carson McCullers told her medical counselor and friend, Dr. Mary Mercer, in 1957 upon the failure of her play, *The Square Root of Wonderful*.[1] The author was still recovering from the trauma suffered upon the death of her mother two years earlier, and the repercussions from her husband's suicide continued to impose themselves upon her creative life. At this point, to write at all was difficult for McCullers.

"No, you haven't," replied the doctor, a child psychiatrist, who assured her that she would find her soul in her work and urged her to keep writing. McCullers had worked intermittently for many years on a long manuscript that she kept putting aside when other tales intruded. Letters that she wrote at Yaddo Artists Colony in 1942 reveal that she was working then not only on *The Member of the Wedding*, which she interrupted to write *The Ballad of the Sad Café*, but also on "The Pestle," whose elusive theme developed eventually into the novel *Clock Without Hands*.

In 1951 McCullers told a reporter that she had had a theme in mind for the past ten years that concerned "how much responsibility . . . a person may take on himself."[2] Two years later she informed an Italian magazine editor who was preparing to publish a segment of "The Pestle" as a work in progress that it was about "good and evil, prejudice, and the affirmation of the dignity of life."[3] McCullers spoke of the "severe moral suffering" of impending death that "brings out a person's most extreme qualities" and said that the new work would introduce her concern for "response and responsibility—[for] man toward his own *livingness,*" a word that she coined for the tale and applied to herself as well. The author insisted fiercely on the determination of her characters to face up to their aloneness, to make moral choices, and thus to achieve the identity that was "rightfully theirs."

Important to the conception of this novel in both theme and event were the countless hours that the author herself had spent years earlier in philosophical debates with her fellow artists with whom she lived in the old brownstone in Brooklyn Heights (New York) during her various estrangements from her husband. McCullers had already handily demonstrated in her life the freedom that came from taking responsibility for her actions and was ripe for W. H. Auden's urgings that she read—and embrace—the teachings of Søren Kierkegaard.[4] Consequently, in 1957, with *The Member of the Wedding* well behind her (both as a novel and a play), the omnibus edition of her collected works published, her ill-fated play *The Square Root of Wonderful* no longer a concern, McCullers returned once more to her "Pestle" manuscript, determined to finish it, then to move on to something else. *Clock Without Hands,* published at last on September 18, 1961, was tangible proof that her creative spirit was intact.[5] Dedicated to Mary Mercer, the novel was McCullers's profession of faith, as well as an extended statement of her existentialist leanings. Just as surely as she was Mick and Singer, Penderton and Ellgee Williams, Amelia and Cousin Lymon, Frankie and John Henry, during the gestation and actual writing of the books in which she gave them life, so, too, was McCullers the three principal characters in *Clock Without Hands,* for whom choices were essential in their respective existential crises.

In anticipation of a cool reception of the novel by critics, Tennessee Williams informed readers in a piece of his own in *Saturday Review* that, despite McCullers's great personal adversity, the novel was "set on paper as indelibly as if it had been carved in stone . . . [with] all the stature, nobility of spirit, and profound understanding of the lonely searching heart that make her, in my opinion, the greatest living author of our country, if not of the world."[6]

Unlike the tight structure of McCullers's earlier book-length works, each having three or four parts with clearly established boundaries, *Clock Without Hands* is composed of thirteen loosely overlapping chapters that are fairly equally distributed among three of the four main characters: J. T. Malone, a forty-year-old druggist who learns that he is dying of leukemia; Jester Clane, who was orphaned at birth and now, at age seventeen, is bent upon getting at the truth behind the mysteries in his life; and Jester's eighty-five-year-old grandfather, Judge Fox Clane, a militant white supremacist. The fourth principal character, Sherman Pew, is a handsome black youth with slate-blue eyes who is determined to learn the source of his white blood and to become his new self in the process. In his various relationships with each of the other characters, Sherman weaves in and out—sometimes as shadow, sometimes full body—until he comes into his own in the last two chapters of the book.[7]

Also, unlike the earlier books, there is no single central event holding the action together in *Clock Without Hands*. Rather, three of its principal characters—Malone, Jester, and Sherman—are more conscious than their predecessors of making things happen, and they assume responsibility for their choices. Increasingly, they suffer anguish and alienation as they become aware of the lack of a meaningful purpose in their lives, and, in the process, attempt to effect their own redemptions. Two of them die in the course of the story. The fourth major character, the deceitful and narcissistic Judge, disintegrates into irredeemable racial bigotry and hopeless senility, unable to make an existential choice.

"Death is always the same, but each man dies in his own way," observes McCullers in her omniscient authorial voice at the novel's opening (1). She informs the reader that when one learns that it is his destiny to suffer, he accepts it as his single, unique task. No one can relieve him of his suffering or suffer in his place. His unique opportunity lies in the way he bears his burden. Such existential truths underlie every important action and decision in the novel.

J. T. Malone—with whom the author most closely identifies, and who is the best developed character—cannot bear the thought of dying in his fragmented state of superficial living, since he has been what he thinks of as a "yes man" and thus has but "half lived." Malone's struggle with his soul is more important and fierce than his struggle with leukemia or any other formidable adversary he had encountered in the past. It is this dilemma from which McCullers drew her title. Malone watches a "clock without hands," knowing that he must die, but not when; thus, he wrestles with his soul and tries to live every day as though it is his last.

Conversely, Jester Clane and Sherman Pew are just beginning to live. Jester, a fledgling pilot, flew his solo flight the very morning that the immediate action in the novel begins. The youth's plane is a Moth, an apt symbol for one who is emerging from his chrysalis. Jester decides that he can no longer put off confronting the mystery of the death of his father, which he perceives as the missing link that will enable him to establish his true purpose in life, and thus to begin living at last. What Jester must discover is that his father, a lawyer, had committed suicide (shortly before his only child was born) because he failed to defend successfully an innocent man accused of murder, a black man who was subsequently executed for the crime. This man was Sherman's father. Moreover, during the course of the trial, Jester's father fell in love with the woman whose lover he was defending, a woman whose hate he incurred upon the jury's guilty verdict. To compound the tragedy was Judge Clane's mockery of justice (as the presiding judge) by siding with the prosecuting attorney.

Jester has little knowledge of, or interest in, his mother, who died in childbirth; rather, it is his father who intrigues him. Sherman, on the other hand, dreams of his mother and wants desperately to know her, having been abandoned as a newborn baby on a church pew (hence his name). The youth yearns for confirmation that he was conceived when his white father raped his black mother (for surely that must be how it happened, he reasons). "Who am I?" demands Sherman repeatedly until he discovers his "horrible truth" while poking into the Judge's files, to which he has access as Fox Clane's amanuensis. Sherman's white blood comes not from his hated father, but from his mother. Moreover, he learns that his black father loved his mother and had killed his mother's despicable husband in self-defense. Malone, Jester, and Sherman all achieve their identity through engagement and moral choice. Only the Judge, a hopeless creator/victim of his time and environment, is beyond redemption. McCullers's ultimate challenge in the novel was to lift the grief-stricken Malone from his existential vacuum—a zone of loneliness unrelieved by his wife, minister, customers, and friends—to existential affirmation.

Whereas *The Ballad of the Sad Café* stands as McCullers's testimony to her belief in the inevitable failure of *eros, Clock Without Hands* exemplifies her faith in the ultimate victory of *agape*.[8] Kierkegaard had insisted that such love was possible "because of the other's need of love." Echoing the philosopher's feelings, McCullers felt that love in its purest state was a matter of loving unaltered by not being loved in return, and that one's truth was a matter of faith, of hope, not fact or a jarring confrontation with reality. At the root of all of her writings in one form or another was her belief in mankind's need for a universal Christian—or brotherly—love. "The further I go into my own work and the more I read of those I love, the more aware I am of the dream and the logic of God, which indeed is a Divine collusion," she insisted.[9] Similarly, McCullers's acknowledgment of the paradox of man's dual existence and the harmony of dream and logic enabled her to combine imagination and reality in her writing. It is the "imagination [that] combines memory with insight, combines reality with the dream," she said.[10] For McCullers, it was the striving that counted. "Reality alone has never been that important to me," she said. "Too many facts impede intuition."[11]

Although she held no consistent stance on the existence or nonexistence of God in her fiction, those who knew her best noted that her concerns for the weak, helpless, and "unlovables" were in line with the social ethics of Christianity. According to Lamar Smith, her brother, and to many others who knew her during the last twenty years of her life, McCullers never stopped thinking of herself as a Christian, no matter what she thought of the organized church and orthodox dogma, or how much she satirized it in her fiction.[12] Her disquietude, so far as the church was concerned, was over its disparity between profession and practice. This disparity is underlined effectively in her fictional portrait of the First Baptist Church in the town, the church to which Malone belongs (that doubtless had its origins in the author's childhood memories of her own church in Columbus, Georgia). In its pursuit of power and money, Malone's church has lost its purpose of awakening members to their spiritual being and fulfilling their various religious needs. McCullers depicted its pastor as a folksy churchman whose analogies from the pulpit are drawn lightly from the nonsecular domain and the sports and business world of contemporary society. The more often that the dying druggist attends church, the more estranged from its ritual and fellow-members he becomes. When at last he visits the minister at home to "get tanked up" on the Holy Sacraments (154), the embarrassed clergyman offers platitudes that send him fleeing into the darkness.

In addition to his distrust of the church, Malone has an aversion to most of the customers in his drug store. Moreover, he shuns any intimacy with his wife, whose crass materialism over the years has intensified his loneliness. Knowing that he is dying physically—as well as emotionally and spiritually—Malone survives for a time in a "curious vacuum," surrounded by talk of his daughter's prom, Tommy's violin recital, a wedding cake, and countless other activities that swirl "about him as dead leaves ring the center of a whirlpool" and leave him "curiously untouched" (9). Judge Clane, whom Malone considers his friend, makes a feeble effort to comfort him by relating endless tales of his own illnesses from which he has recovered and by assuring Malone that his disease is not serious.

In his world of impending doom, the druggist is obsessed with the passage of time. He becomes enraged when the jeweler cannot regulate his watch to railroad time, and as he touches various material objects, he is repelled by the idea that they will exist when he is gone. The ancient stone pestle that he has held a thousand times in the fellowship of work "mocks him" with its look of indestructibility (23). Perhaps the greatest impetus to Malone's unaccustomed reflections on the loss of time and self is his chance reading of Kierkegaard's *Sickness Unto Death,* which prompts him to commit to memory a passage that impresses him: "The greatest danger, that of losing one's own self, may pass off quietly as if it were nothing; every other loss, that of an arm, a leg, five dollars, a wife, etc., is sure to be noticed" (147). This passage forces Malone to try to figure out just how (and *where*) he had "lost" himself. Although it seemed that there was no particular time that he regretted marrying his wife Martha, he knew that "regret" or "disappointment" was there. So, too, had there been no particular occasion that had prompted him to ask: "Is this all there is of life?" Yet he knew that he had asked it implicitly many times. "No, he had not lost an arm, or a leg, or any particular five dollars," he realized, "but little by little he had lost his own self" (149). Thus, it was Malone's knowledge of his imminent death, observed McCullers's omniscient narrator, that quickened his "livingness." The dying man cannot quite comprehend its reality, yet he feels a "sense of ubiquitous unreality" in life itself. He sees no order or conceivable design in the world of incongruities through which he must blunder now in his approach to death. In this respect, Malone resembles Captain Penderton, who "suddenly began to live" during his wild ride on Firebird when he was sure that he would die (once believing that death was certain, Penderton was able to see things as though for the first time). Of all of McCullers's despairing characters, only Captain Penderton rivals Malone in his profound sense of moral aloneness. So, too, does life take on a new awareness for Malone.

To McCullers, Malone's real sickness is not leukemia, but existential despair; thus, for his remaining fifteen months of life he feels driven to search for answers to questions that he had never raised previously. To outwit his wretchedness becomes his monomania. For a time, material possessions represent security. He buys new suits and expensive dental bridges and figures his assets again and again. His pharmacy becomes a welcome retreat in that it represents safety and reality. Finally, as he fingers a bottle of sleeping pills and pictures himself "like a plodding old mule going round and round a sorghum mill," Malone makes an existential choice. He would rather surrender life voluntarily than compromise some higher value (115). His weak suicide attempt fails, however, for instead of dying from the drug overdose, he simply falls into a deep sleep. McCullers implies that Malone is not yet ready to die since he still has not learned *how* to live.

His chance comes—his true moment of choice—when he draws the marked slip of paper designating him to be the instrument of the fire bombing of Sherman Pew's house, and he refuses. "Gentlemen, I am too near death to sin . . . to murder. . . . I don't want to endanger my soul," the druggist confesses (224–225). He has learned, too, that his friend, the Judge, is a central figure among those who plot to undo Sherman's integration of their white neighborhood by blowing up his home. Malone's ultimate epiphany comes in his awareness that he is dying, finally, and his former revulsions give way to a strange lightness and exaltation.

Meanwhile, the tale's focus has shifted intermittently upon Jester Clane, the Judge, and Sherman Pew. When Jester looks at an old painting of a shack on the edge of a peach orchard, he envisions, instead, a pink mule and explains to his grandfather that the picture can be taken as a symbol: "All my life I've seen things like you and the family wanted me to see them. And now this summer I don't see things as I used to—and I have different feelings, different thoughts" (30). Likewise, Jester himself, uncomfortable with tradition, can be viewed as a representative of the New South.

One of Jester's "pink mules" is Sherman Pew, to whom he has been vaguely attracted sexually since their first chance encounter. When the Judge accuses Jester of "having no passion," the youth attributes his passionless state to being a virgin, a condition that he thinks of as his "secret defeat" (42). Whereas Jester had fancied himself "in love" before, until meeting Sherman he had never known passion. When Sherman demands to know why his new acquaintance keeps using the word *passionately,* McCullers's authorial voice intercedes in a style reminiscient of that in the lover/beloved passage in *The Ballad of the Sad Café*:

> Jester, who had been drunk all evening and for the first time with passion, could not answer. For the passion of first youth is lightly sown but strong. It can spring into instant being by a song heard in the night, a voice, the sight of a stranger. Passion makes you daydream, destroys concentration on arithmetic, and at the time you most yearn to be witty, makes you feel like a fool. In early youth, love at first sight, that epitome of passions, turns you into a zombie. . . . Jester felt that if he touched Sherman it would lead to a mortal sin, but what the sin was, he didn't know. He was just careful not to touch him and watched him with the zombie eyes of passion (81–82).

Second only to the black youth's need to know his mother is his yearning for friends. Sherman lies outrageously to Jester in an attempt to enhance his own sense of belonging. Like Benedict Mady Copeland, the black doctor in *The Heart Is a Lonely Hunter,* Sherman does not "fit in" with his race, yet vibrates with every injustice his people have suffered. Verily, who is the Judge's black servant, tells Sherman: "Just because you have them blue eyes is no reason to act so high and mighty. You nigger like the rest of us. You just had a white pappy who passed on them blue eyes to you, and that's nothing to put on airs about" (165). Because of Sherman's slate-blue eyes and his affected speech, the white community, too, considers him an "uppity nigger." Like Honey Brown in *The Member of the Wedding*—who was left "eternally unsatisfied" because

God had not "finished" him—so, too, must Sherman live estranged from both worlds. Like Mick Kelly and many other characters in McCullers's fictional ménage, Sherman sees himself damned because he has been "tricked" or "cheated" (212).

When at last he discovers his true identity, as well as Judge Clane's role in his father's death, Sherman broods darkly over his race and is determined to rebel in some significant way that will make the white community regret its immoral actions. Each insubordinate act, however, terrifies him; moreover, he is even more distressed when he realizes that his violations of the various unwritten laws governing black people in the South go largely unnoticed. Finally, to address his grievance more directly, Sherman substitutes water for insulin in the daily injections he gives the Judge. He is appalled that nothing extraordinary happens to the Judge. He neither gets sick nor dies, and on the fourth day Sherman resumes the proper insulin dosage, reasoning that it would be better to kill the Judge outright if he wanted him dead to insure the deed's being recognized by all as a political act of murder. To attract the attention he craves, Sherman rents a house in a white neighborhood, furnishes it on credit, buys a piano and a new wardrobe, and awaits his fate.

Meanwhile, haunted by his sexual ambivalence, Jester avoids the druggist's daughter (who is in love with him) and skulks outside Madame Reba's whorehouse trying to summon up his flagging spirits to go inside. When he finally does lose his virginity to a prostitute, he imagines Sherman—who has repeatedly rebuffed his awkward overtures—to be his sexual partner. His passion inspired by Sherman gives way, eventually, to an abiding love, a trust-filled friendship, that poses no sexual threat to either of them. In his new self-awareness, Jester stops dreaming of performing such impossible deeds as saving Marilyn Monroe from a Swiss avalanche, receiving a hero's welcome in a ticker tape parade, and dying in the act of saving Sherman from a mob. Instead, he begins dreaming—literally dreaming—of solving the mystery surrounding his father. Finally, upon learning the truth regarding his father's fight for justice, Jester discovers himself as well. "He was his father's son and he was going to be a lawyer," declares McCullers's narrator (204).

Yet before the youth can achieve the maturation he desires, he must develop a keener sense of social responsibility, an achievement that evolves, ultimately, through an act of violence in which he inadvertently participates. Jester's new awareness occurs after Sherman is the victim of a racist bombing. Having overheard in Malone's drugstore the plot to kill Sherman, Jester had tried to warn him, but the youth paid no attention, his elation inspired by the imminence of danger and buoyed by his newly acquired sense of accomplishment. Sherman's actual murderer is Sammy Lank, the "poor white" (and father of five) whose house is next door to the one Sherman had rented. When Jester learns that Lank is the perpetrator of the bombing, he invites him to go flying, a gesture Lank attributes to his new status as "hero" to the white community. Jester plans to kill his passenger either by shooting him (he takes a loaded pistol with him) or crashing the plane and killing himself as well. From his vantage high in the sky, however, Jester surveys the earth and reflects that a "town, even Milan, is symmetrical, exact as a small gray honeycomb, complete" and that the "surrounding terrain seems designed by a law more just and mathematical than the laws of property and bigotry" (233). He realizes as never before that from such a height one does not "see man and the details of his humiliation," and, moreover, that the "whole earth from a great distance means less than one long look into a pair of human eyes. Even the eyes of the enemy" (234). Jester perceives that he can ease his despair and sense of isolation only through a selfless expression of human love or compassion. Like Amelia Evans in *The Ballad of the Sad Café,* who discovered that it was "better to take in . . . [one's] mortal enemy than face the terror of living alone," so, too, does Jester realize that "his odyssey of passion, friendship, love, and revenge" is over (234).

Most of the critics who reviewed *Clock Without Hands* immediately after its publication—and who knew McCullers's earlier work—concurred that her career as a writer was over, also. Irving Howe, writing for the *New York Times Book Review,* objected to the novel's overall structure and its "vague symbolic scheme." He faulted it, too, for what he termed the "lethargic flatness" of its prose.[13] In a similarly negative critique, Louis D. Rubin, Jr., observed that the book was "confusing" because of the way in which McCullers approached the political and social issues. It was as though she had decided "to write a novel 'about' the segregation issue, and fashioned her people entirely with this issue in mind. The result is not a novel but a tract," concluded Rubin.[14] Donald Emerson criticized McCullers for what he saw as an attempt to make her characters "stand for the whole South" and called her "fumbling and uncertain when she attempts a social paradigm."[15] On the other hand, Gore Vidal—who considered McCullers a "genius" and said so in his review[16]—declared that her prose was "one of the few satisfying achievements of our second-rate culture. . . . Of all of the Southern writers, she is the most likely to endure."[17]

Recent criticism of *Clock Without Hands* has focused on such topics as the characters' "fascination with language" and the "ultimate mysteries" that the characters seek to unravel *through* language. In the introduction to her article entitled " 'Fixed in an Inlay of Mystery': Language and Reconciliation in Carson McCullers' *Clock Without Hands,*" Lynn Veach Sadler elaborated on this "fascination of language," saying that "the novel is about the blurring of such distinctions as Black and White in a common identity that appreciates language as a *human* institution and about the role language plays in reconciling us with our humanity."[18] Critics in general faulted McCullers for having no unifying single principal character and for her characterizations of Sherman Pew and the Judge (viewed largely as caricatures rather than as fully rounded characters), for her carelessness of style, for her stereotypical depiction of contemporary youth, and for her preoccupation with death. Clifton Snider, taking a contrary stance, wrote admiringly of McCullers's achievement in *Clock Without Hands* for having dealt so convincingly with death and dying in accordance with modern psychology (in a manner confirmed several years later by Elisabeth Kubler-Ross in *On Death and Dying).* Snider also interpreted the novel in accord with the ideas of Carl Jung.[19]

Despite the novel's being more often than not remembered as the unfortunate end to a brilliant writing career, it remains today an inspiring manifestation of the author's own existential will to live and to write a notable work despite great adversity.

Notes

1. Jordan Massee to Virginia Spencer Carr, interview, New York City, 24 July 1971.

2. McCullers to J. K. Hutchens, "On an Author," *New York Herald Tribune Books* (17 June 1951): 2.

3. "Editor's Introduction," to "The Pestle" [Chapter 1 of *Clock Without Hands*], *Botteghe Obscure*, 11 (1953): 226–246; also *Mademoiselle* 37 (July 1953): 44–45, 114–118.

4. W. H. Auden to Carr, interview, Hinterholz, Austria, 14 Sept. 1973.

5. *Clock Without Hands* (Boston: Houghton Mifflin, 1946). Page references within the text are to this edition.

6 Tennessee Williams, "The Author," *Saturday Review*, 44 (23 Sept. 1961): 14–15.

7. Most of the characters are introduced in the first chapter, but at the center of each chapter are the following principal characters: Malone: chapters 1, 3, 6, and 8; Judge Clane: chapters 2 (shared almost equally with Jester), 5, 9, and 10; Jester: chapters 4, 7, and 11; Sherman: chapters 12 and 13.

8. McCullers, "The Flowering Dream: Notes on Writing" in *The Mortgaged Heart*, ed. Margarita G. Smith (Boston: Houghton Mifflin, 1971), 281. Further citations are to this edition.

9. "The Flowering Dream," 282.

10. "The Flowering Dream," 279.

11. "The Flowering Dream," 276.

12. Lamar Smith to Carr, interview, Perry, Fla., 3 Oct. 1970.

13. Irving Howe, *New York Times Book Review*, (17 Sept. 1961): 5.

14. *The Sewanee Review* 64 (Summer 1962): 509.

15. Donald Emerson, "The Ambiguities of *Clock Without Hands*," *Wisconsin Studies* 3 (Fall 1962): 16.

16. Gore Vidal to Aimee Alexander, letter, 28 Oct. 1970. See also Carr, *The Lonely Hunter: A Biography of Carson McCullers* (New York: Doubleday, 1975), 144.

17. "The World Outside," *The Reporter* 25 (28 Sept. 1961): 50–52.

18. Lynn Veach Sadler, " 'Fixed in an Inlay of Mystery': Language and Reconciliation in Carson McCullers' *Clock Without Hands*," *Pembroke Magazine* 20 (1988): 49.

19. Clifton Snider, "On Death and Dying: Carson McCullers's *Clock Without Hands*," *The Markham Review* 2 (Spring 1982): 41–43.

CHAPTER EIGHT

The Short Fiction

McCullers was a much-acclaimed author and playwright both in America and abroad when her omnibus edition, *"The Ballad of the Sad Café": The Novels and Short Stories of Carson McCullers,* appeared a few weeks after *The Member of the Wedding* closed its long and successful run on Broadway. Although all of the stories (with the exception of "A Domestic Dilemma") had appeared in such magazines as *The New Yorker, Mademoiselle,* and *Harper's Bazaar,* they had never before been brought together in a single volume. Thus, with her three novels, a novella, and six short stories published in a single volume, McCullers was able to reach new readers. Reviewers and scholars alike praised her mastery of the short story and continued to commend her skill as a novelist. Pleased by the book's critical reception, Houghton Mifflin brought out a year later (1952) still another collected edition of McCullers's work, *"The Ballad of the Sad Café" and Collected Short Stories,* which included the novella and the same short stories that had appeared in the original volume, but excluded the novels since they had become readily available in paperback. A reprint edition, published in 1955, included a new story, "The Haunted Boy."

McCullers's posthumous collection, *The Mortgaged Heart* (1971), contained three stories that had not been collected previously ("Correspondence," "Art and Mr. Mahoney," and "Who Has Seen the Wind?") and a handful of apprentice stories that had never been published. It also included many of McCullers's nonfiction pieces and a half dozen poems. Nothing else was published of McCullers except reprint editions and foreign translations of individual works until a much needed new volume, *Collected Stories of Carson McCullers: Including "The Member of the Wedding" and "The Ballad of the Sad Café,"* appeared in 1987.[1]

In tale after tale, regardless of its date of composition, the conflicts depicted by McCullers are intensified by the "immense complexity of love," a phrase that the author coined for one of her most successful short stories, "A Domestic Dilemma."[2] Such love may be between a husband and his wife, an adolescent piano pupil and her teacher, a simple boy and a male cousin he idolizes, a "haunted" youth and his suicidal mother, a seemingly indifferent mother and her tubercular daughter, a jockey and his injured friend, a young girl "in love with a wedding" (or enamored of a Brazilian pen pal who never writes back), an Amazonian woman and a hunchback dwarf, and countless other fictional potential conjoinings that never quite materialize. Most of the latent love relationships in

McCullers's short fiction never reach maturity, and for good reason. As her narrator expressed it in *The Ballad of the Sad Café* (and evident, as well, throughout her writings), "The value and quality of any love is determined solely by the lover himself," and such myopic vision by its very nature destines one's love to go unnoticed or bitterly unrequited (216).[3]

To McCullers, a lover was always vulnerable unless he loved someone—or some thing—from whom he expected nothing in return. In "A Tree. A Rock. A Cloud," a beery tramp confides to a pink-eared newspaper boy, a stranger to him, his "science of love," which he conceived after being abandoned by his wife.[4] The tramp's sterile formula has led him to love things that cannot love back—first, a goldfish, then a tree, a rock, a cloud. But he invites the catcalls of mill workers in the all-night café in which he accosts the child and tells him: "Son! Hey Son! . . . I love you" (124–125). Despite his declaration, the tramp knows that he can walk out alone into the predawn silence and never see his so-called "beloved" again. Loving a woman is the "last step" to his science, he tells the boy. "I go cautious. And I am not quite ready yet" (132). The reader feels intuitively that the dissolute tramp will never be ready for the final step. He will not risk again his vulnerability to *eros*.

Whereas all of McCullers's novels are set in the South, only six of her short stories—"A Tree. A Rock. A Cloud," "Art and Mr. Mahoney," "The Haunted

Boy," "The March," and two apprentice pieces, "Breath from the Sky" and "The Aliens"—make such a setting explicit. At least ten of her stories have obvious settings in the North, and three of her earliest stories ("Sucker," "Like That," and "The Orphanage") have settings that could be anywhere (although the characters, dialogue, and events offer a kind of southern authenticity to the setting, which could well be McCullers's hometown in Georgia or the fictional towns in which *The Heart Is a Lonely Hunter* and *The Member of the Wedding* are set). Her characters who do, in fact, live in the North are often transplanted southerners whose home region remains a memory of pain and anguish.

Despite the acclaim of McCullers's short fiction over the years, little criticism was devoted to the work as a whole until 1978, when Robert Phillips's excellent critical discussion, "Freaking Out: The Short Stories of Carson McCullers" added a new dimension to McCullers scholarship.[5] Phillips demonstrated that most of the characters in her short stories behave quite normally on the surface, yet suffer an "inner freaking-out." Though they exhibit none of the vagaries or physical grotesqueries common to the characters in her longer works, they are immobilized as "spiritual isolates of circumstance."[6]

Another significant characteristic unique to the short stories is the way in which McCullers transformed her personal reality into fiction. Whereas readers who know something of McCullers's girlhood in Georgia (or who knew the author personally) can recognize readily the autobiographical elements in the novels—especially in her depiction of Mick Kelly, Frankie Addams, and Jester Clane—the self-portraits in her short fiction are more cleverly disguised. On the other hand, McCullers's husband appears almost full cloth in three of the short stories: "Instant of the Hour After," "Who Has Seen the Wind?" and "A Domestic Dilemma." In the novels, Reeves McCullers can be recognized only in the characterization of Jake Blount.

The most prevalent theme in the novels—rejection or unrequited love—repeats itself, as one might expect, in her short fiction. McCullers's characters must learn again and again the lesson of *eros,* just as their creator herself had to learn it many times—and to live with it—over the years. The theme is firmly established in her apprentice story, "Sucker."[7] *Sucker* is the nickname of a gullible twelve-year-old boy who idolizes his older cousin, Pete, in whose home he has lived for many years, his parents having been killed in a car accident. Pete, who narrates the tale in an effort to come to grips with Sucker's evolvement into a hardened preadolescent, presents a truism that becomes a refrain, as it were, throughout McCullers's fiction: "If a person admires you a lot you despise him and don't care . . . it is the person who doesn't notice you that you are apt to admire"(2). Pete was in love with Maybelle, a popular older girl who took a casual interest in him until her head was turned by a boy with a yellow roadster. She admits to the crestfallen Pete early in the story that she has "never cared a rap" about him, and he, in turn, attacks Sucker: "Nobody cares anything about you! And just because I felt sorry for you sometimes and tried to act decent don't think I give a damn about a dumb-bunny like you . . . a dumb Sucker" (8).

To cope emotionally with his cousin's betrayal, the boy assumes a façade of hardness (much as Bubber Kelly does in *The Heart Is a Lonely Hunter* when his sister Mick tries to frighten him with thoughts of Sing Sing and an electric chair "just his size"), and it is Pete who yearns to undo the damage. But it is too late. Sucker looks at him in a "new hard way" and insists upon being called by his real name *Richard.* Sucker's physical growth burgeons during the three months immediately following his fall from innocence, and the physiological changes are matched by psychological ones. Richard acts tough and hard with his friends, and when they come to the room he still shares with Pete, the older youth laments that even the room is no longer his: "He [Sucker] sprawls across the bed in those long corduroy pants with the suspenders and just stares at me with that hard, half sneering look. I don't care a flip for Maybelle or any particular girl any more and it's only this thing between Sucker and me that is the trouble now" (9).

McCullers wrote "Sucker" when she was seventeen and trying to deal with her own trauma of what she saw as abandonment upon learning that her piano teacher's husband was being transferred to a distant infantry fort—a move that meant that she would have to continue her lessons with someone else. In her eyes, the entire Tucker family was *her* family, and she was devastated. Not since the acute jealousy that her infant sister had aroused by her "intrusion" (as McCullers saw it) into the Smith household at birth had she felt so personally undermined. The characters whose shrill cries of being "cheated" resound repeatedly throughout McCullers's fiction certainly owe much of their genesis to McCullers's response to the Tucker family's move.

Frances, the main character in "Wunderkind"—and Sucker, her counterpart—are the earliest versions of McCullers's countless adolescents who are torn in time, dislodged from the safety of childhood, yet not ready, either, for the world of adults. "Wunderkind," written a few months after "Sucker," was another early attempt by McCullers to objectify her wretched perception of having been renounced.[8] Frances, more boldly autobiographical than Sucker, is a young piano pupil who perceives that she is no longer a *wunderkind* and wrestles with what she should do about it. In this tale it is the piano teacher who, ultimately, is abandoned. Important to the initiation theme in "Wunderkind" is the reader's recognition of the paradoxical nature of love and human charity. Frances teeters between adolescence and maturity in an unsuccessful struggle to play for her teacher (whom she loves), with the passion, sensitivity, and technique she had shown when they first began working together. Equally responsible for the dilemma is Mr. Bilderbach, Frances's teacher, who resists admitting, because he loves her, that her talent is unpromising. His pupil seems like a daughter to him, and he welcomes special opportunities to give her presents, which she views with resentment as "charity." She has no interest in anything but music, and all she can think about is "playing the music as it must be played, bringing out the thing that must be in her, practicing, practicing, playing so that Mister Bilderbach's face lost some of its urging look" (66). Through her teacher, Frances becomes aware not only of her own musical ineptitude, but also of her evolving sexuality. As she strives to please him she is aware that his "deep voice sounded as though it had been straying inside her for a long time. She wanted to reach out and touch his muscle-flexed finger that pointed out the phrases, wanted to feel the gleaming gold band ring and the strong hairy back of his hand" (62).[9]

In an attempt to play another Beethoven *variation*, Frances longs to start the dirge "with subdued viciousness and progress to a feeling of deep, swollen sorrow," but her "hands seemed to gum in the keys like limp macaroni," and she could not even imagine the music (68). "I can't. I don't know why, but I just can't—can't anymore," she whispers, then clutches her belongings—her music, her coat, her mittens and galoshes, the book satchel he had given her for her birthday, everything "from the silent room that was hers"—and flees the house. Frances's painfully acquired self-knowledge leads to her stumbling flight from the master's studio, to which she knows she will never return. The girl's profound sense of loss is shared by her teacher as well, but in their confusion and hurt, neither can admit it. Ironically, when McCullers wrote this story, she was unaware that her actual teacher had felt a great sense of abandonment and loss over having to leave the young Carson Smith behind in Columbus.[10]

Some twenty-five years after its publication, McCullers reflected that just as Tennessee Williams had written *The Glass Menagerie* as a memory play, so, too, had she written "Wunderkind" as a memory, but not the "reality of the memory"; rather, it was a "foreshortening of that memory. It was about a young music student. I didn't write about my real music teacher—I wrote about the music we studied together because I thought it was truer. The imagination is truer than the reality."[11] When McCullers wrote these words, she had already written *The Member of the Wedding* (both as a novel and a play), and she and her piano teacher had attended the play together in New York, an occasion that led to their reconciliation. McCullers's declaration to her teacher that she was giving up her plans to become a concert pianist in order to become a writer was her recognition no doubt, that her precious musical talent either was waning or had been misjudged. She had been a star struck too high, for whom the fall now was inconsolably painful.

"Like That," another apprentice tale, was purchased by Whit Burnett for *Story* magazine in 1936, along with "Wunderkind," but it remained unpublished until it surfaced years later in the *Story* archives at Princeton University. Burnett felt that a story whose central incident revolved around a young woman's first menstruation should be suppressed until "more liberal times."[12]

Similar in theme and narrative mode to "Sucker," "Like That" is an interior monologue by a pubescent girl about her older sister's coming of age ("Sis" is eighteen and "grown-up now"), but the real initiation is the narrator's. If being grown-up means acting "like that," she wants nothing to do with it. "I know there's no way I can make myself stay thirteen all my life," she says, "but I know I'd never let anything really change me at all—no matter what it is" (56). She recalls the satisfying years of growing up—of making fudge, playing three-handed bridge with their brother (who at eighteen is also experiencing growing pains), and sharing holidays, books, and secrets with her brother and sister before her sudden awareness that "growing up" alters everything. She speaks painfully of her discovery that "Sis" had just "started with what every big girl has each month," and frightened and angry, she tells "Sis": "Anybody can tell. Right off the bat. . . . It looks terrible. I wouldn't ever be like that" (54).

Later in the tale (marked by a five-year interval), the narrator makes a new discovery. She has just surmised that her sister has undergone a new initiation—a sexual one—that further confirms her coming of age. The younger girl does not know exactly what has happened, but she hears the "sharpness" in her sister's voice, is troubled by her sister's sad looks and silent, terrible weeping following a date with Tuck, a college student, and recognizes that her relationship with her sister has changed permanently. The name *Tuck* (another echo of *Mary Tucker,* McCullers's former piano teacher) and the narrator's anguish as a result of the incident reveal a more blatant use of persona and events from the author's own life than usual. Unwilling to forsake childhood, the narrator rides her bicycle, skates, goes to football games, wears bobby socks, withdraws from the group in the basement of the school gym when they begin "telling certain things—about being married and all," vows never to wear lipstick—not "for a hundred dollars"—and declares that she is "hard boiled" and will not "waste her time trying to make Sis like she used to be" (56–57). The child's hostility toward change foreshadows Mick's in *The Heart Is a Lonely Hunter,* and in her pain of conversion, she is a combination of Sucker and Pete.

Still another early memory piece and a more somber initiation tale than the other apprentice pieces is "The Orphanage."[13] McCullers can be taken here, too, for the unidentified narrator of this prosaic slice-of-life that has no plot or character development (and very little movement). Yet there is drama in the tale as the narrator looks back upon an incident that occurred when she was six or seven and had an older friend Hattie, whom she identifies as her "initiator" (36). When the narrator and her cousin Tit (a male cousin her age) promise not to reveal to anyone else what she is going to show them, Hattie retrieves from a closet shelf a "dead pickled baby" in a jar that her brother had brought home "when he was learning to be a drug store man" (38). It was an orphan, she told them. The narrator had always been intrigued by the town's orphanage and often passed it with her grandmother (for it was on the main thoroughfare to downtown), but Hattie's revelation of the "pickled orphan" haunts the narrator and provokes wild, fearful dreams.

McCullers interrupts her tale midway to observe that the "memories of childhood have a strange shuttling quality, and areas of darkness ring the spaces of light . . . [like] clear candles in an acre of night, illuminating fixed scenes from the surrounding darkness" (37). Even though the children whom the narrator saw playing on their swings and exercise bars were orphans, they had each other as an "assorted whole" (39). McCullers's coda of the chain gang in *The Ballad of the Sad Café* became her telescoped treatise on the same subject. Another version of being an envious outsider watching children at play was rendered more directly in McCullers's essay "The Flowering Dream: Notes on Writing." The frustration felt by a character who has been excluded from things in which he/she desperately wants to share is treated again and again in McCullers's fiction, just as the author herself experienced it repeatedly in life.

Yet another early tale of rejection set in the South, but developed quite differently, is "Breath from the Sky," published posthumously—as were these other early pieces—for the first time in *The Mortgaged Heart* (31–39). In "Breath from the Sky," Constance, a fragile girl of fourteen or fifteen, is about to be sent away to a sanitarium in Mountain Heights (Georgia) for treatment for what appears to be advanced tuberculosis.[14] Constance fears that she will never return home and that her younger brother and sister will live out their carefree lives as though she had never existed. Made implicit by the point of view through which the story unfolds is the fact that, regardless of appearances, Constance's mother is not indifferent to her daughter's plight. Rather, the older woman's apparent insensitivity is simply her means of dealing with the tragedy. Ultimately, the story is as much the mother's as it is the ailing daughter's. Not surprisingly, readers of this early tale who lived in Columbus, Georgia, and knew both McCullers and her mother (Marguerite Waters

Smith), readily perceived Constance's mother to be a thinly disguised portrait of the author's own.[15]

Throughout McCullers's canon, it is noteworthy that the children she depicts have no strong emotional ties with their mothers. Lamar Smith believed that his sister "did not want to strip herself 'that bare' and reveal her utter dependency" on their mother. "Sister was too vulnerable," he continued. "She was our mother's favorite child, and somehow my sister Rita and I understood this. We were convinced that Sister was a genius, and that our mother was, also, for letting that genius flower."[16] McCullers's fictional mothers—if they are mentioned at all—either die in childbirth, as does Frankie's in *The Member of the Wedding*; are too preoccupied with helping to support the family when the father cannot, as does Mick's in *The Heart Is a Lonely Hunter*; drink too much, as does Emily Meadows in "A Domestic Dilemma"; or attempt suicide, as does Hugh's in "The Haunted Boy." On the other hand, the fathers in her fiction are treated rather compassionately. Like Mick's and Frankie's fathers, they suffer because they fail to communicate with their daughters, who are only vaguely aware of their sense of loss and appear reticent to deal with them directly.

In "Court in the West Eighties," a long and less well-developed apprentice piece than most of the others in the posthumous collection edited by McCullers's sister, the narrator is an eighteen-year-old university student in New York City who comments upon the people living in the court whom she views from her window. The neighbor who intrigues her most is a red-headed man who keeps milk and crocks of food on his window sill, and who looks out upon the court just as she does. "We were near enough to throw our food into each others' windows, near enough so that a single machine gun could have killed us all together in a flash" (16), observes the narrator, her flair for the dramatic similar to her creator's. When trouble brews among several of the residents of the court, the young woman is certain that the man with the red hair "was the one person able to straighten it out. . . . I had a feeling that nothing would surprise him and that he understood more than most people" (14–15). Despite her ratiocination, the narrator knows that neither she nor the strange man with the red hair could possibly straighten out things for any of them, that one simply lives his own life and endures it. Although the tale is slight and clearly an apprentice piece, it is important to readers of McCullers's first novel in that the narrator and the man she watches are sensitively drawn prototypes of Mick Kelly and John Singer, who were germinating as early as 1935 when McCullers first went north.

Two other stories, "The Aliens" and a fragment identified as "Untitled Piece," are also important early versions of materials that appeared eventually in McCullers's novels (and published for the first time in *The Mortgaged Heart*). One of the earliest prototypes of John Singer is Felix Kerr in "The Aliens." A displaced Jew, Kerr is journeying south by bus to make a home for the family he has left in Europe. The story, which takes place in August of 1935, is actually a dialogue between the Jew and the passenger who sits beside him, a naïve farm boy. The tale remains static until a black woman, who appears "deformed—although not in any one specific limb," gets on the bus; her body as a whole is "stunted, warped and undeveloped" (76). To the Jew, everything about her seems repugnant, and he asks the youth: "What is the matter with her?"

"Who? You mean the nigger?" the youth replies. "Why there's nothing the matter with her. . . . Not that I can see." Bound by the parameters of his farm, the boy is as maimed in his own social perception as the woman is in her physical grotesqueness. Ironically, both the woman and the youth get off the bus at the same stop, inextricably linked by their environment. The youth has unwittingly revealed that he is as isolated in his own region as the wandering Jew is in this foreign land (and as the black woman herself must be)—all three, social pariahs. Alone once more, Kerr, thinking of his wife and their younger daughter who will join him soon, is suddenly stricken with an inconsolable grief for another daughter whose whereabouts and welfare remain a mystery to him.

The fragmented family appears throughout McCullers's canon, a theme she experimented with again and again in her early work. Her longest story, published as "Untitled Piece" in *The Mortgaged Heart,* is important, too, for its seeds that flower later in *The Heart Is a Lonely Hunter.* The tale is told from the point of view of Andrew Leander, who leaves his Georgia home at seventeen for New York City and returns at twenty-one, the full initiate. Like most of McCullers's short fiction, the story is a memory piece concerning Andrew's awakening and his ambivalent feelings toward his family as he gains self-awareness. Andrew has two sisters (Sara and Mick) and no mother, only the young black houseservant Vitalis, who—like Portia in *The Heart Is a Lonely Hunter* and Berenice Sadie Brown in *The Member of the Wedding*—functions as a surrogate. Andrew recalls the sounds, scents, and events in his life when he was on the edge of puberty—a maturation that he and his sister Sara had yearned for, yet tried to forestall. Andrew—whose father is a jeweler—is not only a Mick Kelly figure, but a prototype, as well, of Jake Blount and Dr. Copeland in *The Heart Is a Lonely Hunter.* He is also similar to Harry Minowitz, with whom Mick has her first sexual experience (both Harry and Andrew flee to distant cities after their encounters). But in McCullers's "Untitled Piece," Harry Minowitz is an actual character, a Jew who borrows a workbench from Andrew's father on which to set up his business as a watch repairman. It is the Minowitz of this tale who eventually evolves into John Singer, the deaf-mute.

McCullers's "Untitled Piece" is the best single prototype of any of her longer fiction and affords an intriguing study of the creative process. The reader who is well acquainted with *The Heart Is a Lonely Hunter* can see how McCullers developed her characterizations, used and discarded incidents, reassigned various character traits, and created the tightly controlled structure that was missing from her untitled apprentice work.

Although Andrew is never a fully rounded character—largely because he tells his own rambling story—McCullers succeeded in recreating his distorted vision and slow search for selfhood, punctuated by a series of Joycean epiphanies. Andrew's restless search for identity resembles that of Stephen Daedalus (by this time McCullers had read *Portrait of an Artist as a Young Man*, as well as Joyce's Dubliner tales, and was admittedly influenced by them). Andrew's father is much like the father of Frankie Addams, who works deftly and lovingly at his jeweler's bench, his eyes seeing only the immediate task before him. The "eye that wore the jeweler's glass" is distorted, and the other eye is "squinted almost shut." Although he sometimes stares out at people passing his window on the street, he does not speak to them, nor does he communicate successfully with either Sara or his son (Andrew's father closely resembles the fathers of Mick and Frankie, both of whom owe their genesis to McCullers's father).

After his sexual initiation, Andrew abandons his plans to go to Georgia Tech to study engineering and goes instead to New York City, that spot "on an aerial map . . . far away . . . frozen and delicate" (102). When he returns to the South three years later, his odyssey having come full circle, he is drunk and sick for home.

These apprentice pieces and McCullers's "Outline to 'The Mute' " comprise more than half of *The Mortgaged Heart* and make a significant contribution to the reader's appreciation of her work as a whole. Much of the author's best fiction was germinating during her first three years in New York City before she was married, but she made little attempt to publish what she was writing. In 1939, while living with her husband in Fayetteville, North Carolina, McCullers sent "Sucker" and "Court in the West Eighties" to Maxim Lieber, a New York literary agent who agreed to try to market them for her, and both pieces made the rounds quickly from magazine to magazine without success.[17] Lieber's failure to place "Sucker" worked, eventually, to McCullers's advantage in that she received $1,500 for its publication in *The Saturday Evening Post* in 1963 (in contrast to the $25 she received for her first published story, "Wunderkind").

Other work written for Sylvia Chatfield Bates's fiction workshop at New York University was apparently never submitted by McCullers for publication. Extensive comments by Bates about three such stories that survived through the years in McCullers's personal archives—"Poldi," "Instant of the Hour After," and "Wunderkind"—are reproduced in *The Mortgaged Heart*.

"Poldi" is an engaging tale of unrequited love, but it is less successful than most of the other early pieces. Although the physically unattractive Poldi Klein, a cellist, appears to be the main character, it is the hapless lover Hans (who resembles Sucker in many ways) with whom the reader ultimately sympathizes. Hans—from whose viewpoint the story unfolds—is a grieving, pimply-faced pianist who has loved inordinately the overweight, unattractive cellist for two years without her having the slightest awareness that his devotion is anything more than concern for her well-being. Poldi, on the other hand, has been in love with a succession of men who have little awareness that she even exists. At the story's opening, Hans visits the cellist's studio again, this time determined to confess his feelings and to rescue her from her destitute state (Poldi cannot even afford to repair her damaged instrument); however, before he can convey his feelings, she informs him that she has declared in a note her unbridled love for someone else (then offers countless reasons for the man's silence). When Hans gently reminds her that her new beloved is engaged to marry someone else, Poldi replies: "Yes. But it's a mistake. What would he want with a cow like her?" (24). The neglected Hans realizes that the woman's illusions are essential if she is to survive, and he does what he can to confirm them.

Hans's decision to support the woman's fantasy reinforces the similarities between "Poldi" and McCullers's tale of another musician, "Madame Zilensky and the King of Finland." Madame Zilensky, a composer and piano teacher, becomes a pathological liar in an attempt to escape through fantasy an awareness of her fragmentation in a disordered world. Just as the metronome provides a mechanical tempo for her performance and teaching of music, so, too, do her lies and fantasies impose an illusory order upon her personal life. Madame Zilensky's downfall comes when her supervisor, known only as Mr. Brook, challenges one of her harmless deceptions after she tells him of having seen the King of Finland go by on a sled as she stood in front of a *pâtisserie* in Helsingfors (Helsinki). Later, it occurs to Brook that Finland has never had a king, that the country is a democracy, and he can hardly wait to expose her.

Yet, by stripping the woman of her illusions—unwilling, as it were, to *brook* the lie—Brook strips Madame Zilensky of her soul as well. In this early tale McCullers establishes with no uncertainty her conviction that illusions are essential if one is to endure life's painful realities. When one's dream is ravished by grim ratiocination, the dreamer, too, is destroyed. McCullers, however, does not allow the destroyer to go unpunished. Almost at once Brook experiences a "great commotion of feelings—understanding, remorse, and unreasonable love," and he covers his face with his hands. "Yes. Of course. The King of Finland. And was he nice?" Brook asks the stricken woman (117), but the situation is irreparable.

Whereas the tale appears to focus on the unfortunate woman (as does "Poldi"), the important reversal in the action concerns Brook himself, who is described early in the story as a solitary man who loathes "academic fiddle-faddle" and takes a trip alone to Peru instead of joining his music colleagues in Salzburg. A silent observer, Brook reminds the reader of Biff Brannon, the café owner in *The Heart Is a Lonely Hunter.* He is tolerant of the peculiarities of others and claims even to relish them. In the course of the story, he learns something about himself as well, just as Brannon has his moment of revelation at the novel's close. An hour after Brook had handily dispatched Madame Zilensky, he sits alone in his room, vaguely disquieted, as he grades papers for his counterpoint class. Suddenly he views from the window the neighbor's old Airedale waddling down the street. At first the dog behaves as usual, then inexplicably appears to be "running along backward." That the dog is actually running backward—in a kind of crab or mirror counterpoint—is illusory, and Brook dismisses the phenomenon as impossible. Yet, in destroying the illusions of Madame Zilensky, Brook also fragments himself. The solitary professor may be able to teach and grade counterpoint, but, ironically, he cannot allow counterpoint to exist in his own life. These two dissimilar human beings might have come together contrapuntally in a rare spiritual communion and thus ease their self-estrangement—just as two dissimilar themes or melodies may run counter, yet concurrently, to combine into a harmonious single entity—but the two fragmented halves that they finally represent are too dissonant to make a whole.

"The Sojourner," a more subtle and mature story of unrequited love, is a "remembrance of things past" juxtaposed with the painful present.[18] This lyrical tale has its origins, like so many of McCullers's other stories, in her troubled life with her husband. It, too, employs music in its resolution and deals with displacement and a character's need for order in a disordered society.

John Ferris, from whose point of view the story is told, is a displaced southerner who has come home from Paris to attend the funeral of his father in Georgia. Back in New York City for scarcely twenty-four hours before boarding a plane to return to Paris, he sees his former wife, Elizabeth, quite by chance and follows her briefly without her knowing it. Suddenly, Ferris literally "wheels" from her to distance himself once more from the bittersweet memories interwoven with the "jealousy, alcohol and money quarrels" that had destroyed "fiber by fiber" the "fabric of married love." He had thought himself invulnerable to old emotions, yet seeing her again (when he calls her, she invites him to dinner), meeting her husband and their two beautiful children, hearing her perform at the piano a Bach prelude and fugue (then an elusive melody that he could not place), he was "lost in the riot of past longings, conflicts, ambivalent desires" (144). Elizabeth's playing is interrupted by the maid announcing dinner, and, later, on the plane en route to Paris, Ferris tries to recapture her "singing melody," but it is too late. His self-perception at this moment is that he is suspended between two worlds—an idealized world suggestive of what might have been (symbolized by Elizabeth's music and her face, "a madonna loveliness, dependent of the family ambiance") and his own disordered world, a "succession of cities, of transitory loves; and time, the sinister glissando of the years, time always" (146). Having a lover who was already married to someone else was safe, just as the old tramp's declaration to a strange child—"Son, I love you"—was safe. So long as neither risks his vulnerability, his "science of love" is secure.

"The Sojourner" was singled out by early critics, along with "A Domestic Dilemma," as two of the best stories in McCullers's omnibus collection, *"The Ballad of the Sad Café": The Novels and Stories of Carson McCullers* (1951). Later, McCullers adapted "The Sojourner" for a television drama entitled "The Invisible Wall," which was produced live by the Ford Foundation on "Omnibus Theater."[19]

In "The Haunted Boy," another story of wounded adolescence and rejection set in Georgia, Hugh is haunted by the fear that he will return from school one day and discover his mother lying in a pool of blood on the bathroom floor, just as he had discovered her a few months earlier after a failed suicide attempt that resulted in her being sent to the state mental hospital in Milledgeville. Although the boy's mother has recovered and is back home when the story opens, Hugh cannot forgive his mother for what he sees as her attempt to abandon him. The boy's hostility and sense of guilt drive him to his friend John for succor, but John is insensitive to Hugh's unspoken needs, and, thus, cannot share his burden. Hugh recognizes in his distress, finally, that he hates John, reasoning that "you hate people you have to need so badly!" (156).

Young Hugh's admission reflects the ambivalence of McCullers's own feelings toward her mother, with whom she felt increasingly uncomfortable (in direct proportion to her dependency upon her) after her husband's suicide. Yet in making her protagonist an adolescent boy (a gender disguise that the author employed in much of her fiction), McCullers successfully objectified her ambivalent love-hate-guilt feelings, feelings that she tried repeatedly to suppress in her life and to conceal from her mother. Friends of McCullers who knew her mother may have viewed the tale as a thinly disguised fiction of a "haunted girl." McCullers probably began work on the story in 1954, but the exact date of composition is unknown. Her mother died of a bleeding ulcer in 1955, five months before "The Haunted Boy"—ultimately yet another version of the author's thesis on love presented in *The Ballad of the Sad Café*—was published.[20]

McCullers ends this tale, too, in strange fashion compared to her usual final resolutions. It is Hugh's father who now partially redeems him. Whereas he had distanced himself from his son during his wife's crisis, he now praises Hugh for his courage in accepting the experience and treats him like a grown-up for the first time. "The Haunted Boy" provides one of the few father figures in McCullers's fiction who make any positive impression upon a son or daughter. Although the ending is mawkish and lacks conviction, the reader appreciates the boy's emergence from moral isolation into self-knowledge.

"Correspondence"—McCullers's only story in the epistolary form—is one of McCullers's best and most tightly controlled conversions of life into art. The tale consists solely of four letters from Henky Evans, another Frankie Addams character (though she lives in Darien, Connecticut), who pours out her adolescent heart to a Brazilian pen pal who never writes back. Henky's salutations and closings reveal her growing awareness of failure and rejection as she moves from "Dear Manuel" and "Your affectionate friend, Henky Evans" to "Dear Mr. Garcia" and "Yrs. truly, Miss Henrietta Hill Evans." In her final letter Henky demands to know why the youth had "put his name on the pen pal list" if he did not intend to fulfill his part of the agreement. In a postscript she adds: "I cannot waste any more of my valuable time writing to you" (124). It is unlikely that Henky Evans—who lacks Frankie Addams's resilience—will put her name on a pen pal list again or otherwise risk her vulnerability.

In actuality, McCullers interrupted her work on *The Ballad of the Sad Café* to write this story, one prompted by her husband's failure to answer her letters while she was spending her first summer at Yaddo Artists Colony. As she saw it, Reeves McCullers—like Henky's South American pen pal—had defaulted on his contract. McCullers resolved to waste no more "valuable time" on her marriage and immediately initiated divorce proceedings, having learned that her husband had gone away secretly with their best friend.

"The Jockey," another poignant story of loss that McCullers wrote at Yaddo the same summer that she wrote "Madame Zilensky and the King of Finland" and "Correspondence," was set in Saratoga Springs, a spa town famous for its August races. McCullers went to the flat track several times that summer (1941) and drank cocktails at the Worden Bar, which Saratoga

Springs readers easily recognized as the setting for "The Jockey."[21] The external conflict in this tale is between the jockey Bitsey Barlow—whose description brings to mind that of the hunchback dwarf in *The Ballad of the Sad Café*— and a trio whom he accosts in the restaurant: the owner of the horse that Barlow rode the day of the incident, the horse's trainer, and a bookie. Whether the jockey had ridden to victory that day or lost the race was not the issue, nor does the omniscient narrator comment upon it. What *does* cause concern, and provides the catalyst to the action, is the realization that the jockey's best friend (who rode for the same owner and trainer) will never ride again because of the injuries he sustained in an earlier race. "Libertines," Barlow hisses when he finds the trio at dinner over a sumptuous meal, his impotent rage reminiscent of Jake Blount's in *The Heart Is a Lonely Hunter.* The jockey sees his adversaries as animals incapable of concern for the maimed rider. The trio wants only to *replace* the wounded jockey as quickly as possible. A horse with a broken leg is shot, but the unfortunate jockey in a callous environment is trapped forever, implies McCullers.

The frustrated jockey and his disabled companion have been caught, cheated—like Mick in *The Heart Is a Lonely Hunter* and others in her fictional landscape—because the cards are stacked against them. McCullers continued to rail against the "ironies of fate" as she turned repeatedly during the summer of 1941 from her book-length tale of the hapless Frankie Addams who is hopelessly in love with a wedding, to the writing of short stories concerning unrequited love—artistic achievements from which she could gain more immediate release from her disappointments and frustrations.

A story that McCullers wrote several years later that depicts philistines of a different sort is "Art and Mr. Mahoney," published in *Mademoiselle* and selected by McCullers's sister for inclusion in *The Mortgaged Heart* for its deft detail and sharp satire of provincial manners and the prostitution of art.[22] It is not the title character Mahoney, but his wife, who is the true philistine. Mahoney, once a country boy, now owns a brick yard and mill and is a pillar of society in his small southern town in which the pretentious patrons of little theater plays and concerts wear "chiffon and corsages and decorous dinner jackets" to the high school auditorium and attend what they think of as "gala" receptions. Mahoney can talk handily about abstract art and "repertory" and assume the "proper expression of meek sorrow" at a concert or lecture, having been "well drilled" by his culturally groomed wife. The couple's position in their smalltown world of art and culture seems secure until Mahoney makes his "fatal" mistake: he claps too soon during a Chopin sonata played by Jose Iturbi at the season's opening concert. Mahoney was "so dead sure it was the end that he clapped heartily half a dozen times before he realized, to his horror, that he clapped alone" (136). The man's shame is exceeded only by his wife's humiliation. At a party afterward, an acquaintance of Mahoney's who does not "know a sonata from the *Slit Belly Blues*," yet who has done nothing to provoke ostracism, safely approaches the humiliated offender and declares with "a slow wink of covert brotherhood" that the subscription tickets Mahoney had sold ought to entitle him "to an extra clap" if he wanted one (137).

The tale—told from Mahoney's point of view, yet rendered through an omniscient voice that one takes for McCullers's own—affords the reader scant sympathy for the offender; yet more to the point, the author offers no hope of redemption for Mrs. Mahoney either, who can neither forgive her husband nor recognize her own duplicity in the charade. The woman is ignorantly and permanently entrapped in smug conventionalism, a fate more damning than death itself, suggests McCullers.

The concept of the "immense complexity of love"—a phrase from her short story "A Domestic Dilemma"—surfaces often in McCullers's writings, especially in her domestic tales that reflect aspects of her life with Reeves McCullers. The earliest story of domestic discord, "Instant of the Hour After," was written when the author was nineteen. It depicts a wretched evening in the life of a young husband and wife whose marriage is disintegrating because of his inability to control his drinking. Although the wife (unnamed) loves her husband, she is put off by his torrent of meaningless words and sarcasms when he is drunk. She wonders vaguely what life might have been like had she married their friend Phillip, who often came to their apartment to play chess. McCullers was not married when she wrote this story, but she and Reeves were already living together in New York (he was enrolled at Columbia University, while sporadically trying to write fiction himself).

"Instant of the Hour After" is McCullers's only story in which both the husband and wife drink heavily. The young wife in the tale sees herself entrapped with her husband in a bottle, "skeetering angrily up and down the cold blank glass like minute monkeys" until they collapse, exhausted, "looking like fleshy specimens in a laboratory. With nothing said between them" (46). Despite her teacher's urging that she revise the tale, McCullers chose not to do so, apparently having found the material too painful and personal to attempt to rework it.

The second tale in which marital harmony is disrupted by alcohol is "A Domestic Dilemma."[23] Its tone is reminiscent of "Instant of the Hour After." This time it is the sherry-tippling housewife Emily Meadows who precipitates the conflict. Emily drinks furtively and cannot be trusted with the safe rearing of their two young children. Her husband Martin—from whose point of view the story unfolds—assumes much of the responsibility for the dilemma, for he has uprooted his wife from the south and moved her to an unnamed suburban town on the Hudson River.[24] Homesick and unable to adjust to the "stricter, lonelier mores of the North," Emily stays to herself, reads magazines and murder mysteries, and finds her interior life "insufficient without the artifice of alcohol." Martin has been uneasy about their children ever since Emily, in a state of intoxication, had allowed their infant daughter to slip from her arms while carrying her naked from her bath. Having hired a housekeeper as a result of the accident, the young husband now worries only on Thursday afternoons, the servant's afternoon off. The tale opens on such a Thursday as a domestic crisis is in progress.

Martin has just discovered that Emily had sprinkled red pepper (rather than cinnamon) on the children's buttered toast, then left them alone to eat while she sipped sherry in the bedroom upstairs. After a confrontation with Emily and a drunken scene in the kitchen in front of the children, Martin fixes soup and insists that she eat; then he puts her to bed—his dull hard anger "like a weight upon his chest"—before bathing the children and settling them for the night. His anger rises as he thinks of their vulnerability, and he reflects, too, upon his own youth, which he sees being "frittered by a drunkard's waste." Later, as he undresses for bed and observes his wife in the darkened room in "tranquil slumber," he becomes suddenly overwhelmed by tenderness. He perceives his daughter in the arch of Emily's handsome brow and his son in her chin and high cheekbones. Then, inexplicably and at once, the "ghost of the old anger" and all thoughts of "blame or blemish" vanish, and he slides into bed trying not to awaken his wife. Ultimately, sorrow parallels desire "in the immense complexity of love," and his hand seeks the "adjacent flesh" (157).

"A Domestic Dilemma" aptly demonstrates McCullers's narrative gift for understatement and her ability to handle a story told from a man's point of view that is equally as sensitive and sympathetic as one told from the woman's perspective.

Still another complex tale of love and domestic crisis brought on by alcohol is "Who Has Seen the Wind?"[25] This long tale dealt McCullers considerable pain, too, in the writing. Whereas the alcoholic husband in "Instant of the Hour After" was a young man of twenty, his later counterpart is almost forty. Written exactly twenty years after "Instant of the Hour After," "Who Has Seen the Wind?" is the story of Ken Harris, an author of one successful novel and a bitterly unsuccessful second novel. At this point in his life, Harris cannot write at all, but sits staring at a blank sheet in the typewriter and sporadically alternating *X* and *R* on the keys. At a recent cocktail party he had warned a young writer that a "small, one-story talent" is the "most treacherous thing that God can give" (185). Harris feels betrayed, too, by his wife (who supports him by her editing job in the city) because she refuses to take seriously his repeated urgings that they move to an apple farm, an idyllic dream they had once shared. When she refuses her husband in bed as well, telling him "No. Never again," and pleads with him to seek help for his sickness, he threatens to stab her with her sewing scissors. Harris is desolate when he discovers a few moments later that she has left him alone with his psychotic fears, and he lurches with "luminous lost eyes" into a blinding snowstorm and "the unmarked way ahead." Yet as he stumbles toward his own certain death at the story's end, he stops a policeman to report that his wife is crazy and has just tried to kill him. "She ought to be helped before something awful happens," he instructs.[26]

The parallels that run between the conflict in this story and that which the author experienced as the wife of Reeves McCullers are undeniable. Interestingly enough, however, is the fact that in the last days of their life together it was *Reeves* who spoke to McCullers of bringing life to an end (trying to convince her to participate in a double suicide with him), whereas in the story it is the *wife* who threatens her husband with talk of death. Likewise, in reality, it was McCullers who deserted Reeves definitively (leaving him behind in Paris, where he committed suicide in 1953—three years before this story was published), whereas in this fictional rendering it is *Ken* who runs away.

One final short story, "The March," was published in *Redbook* a few weeks before McCullers's death.[27] A thin civil rights story set in the South, it was not included in either of the posthumous collections of her work. Most readers (if they know it at all) agree that "The March" does not approach the quality of excellence in her other short fiction. She had intended the tale to be the first of a trilogy of short stories, but she was unable to complete the other two before her death.[28] McCullers's best short stories remain those that she wrote during her young womanhood in the 1930s and 1940s.

Notes

1. *Collected Stories of Carson McCullers: Including "The Member of the Wedding" and "The Ballad of the Sad Café"* (Boston: Houghton Mifflin, 1987). All page references within the text are to this edition.

2. "A Domestic Dilemma" was first published in the omnibus edition, *"The Ballad of the Sad Café": The Novels and Stories of Carson McCullers.* (Boston: Houghton Mifflin, 1951) 115–127.

3. "The Ballad of the Sad Café" was first published in *Harper's Bazaar* 77 (Aug. 1943): 72–75, 140–161.

4. "A Tree. A Rock. A Cloud" was first published in *Harper's Bazaar* 76 (Nov. 1942): 50.

5. Robert Phillips, *Southwest Review* 63 (Winter 1978): 65–73.

6. Phillips, 66.

7. "Sucker" was first published in *The Saturday Evening Post* 236 (Sept. 1963): 69–71.

8. "Wunderkind" was first published in *Story* 9 (Dec. 1936): 61–73.

9. See Constance M. Perry, "Carson McCullers and the Female *Wunderkind*," *The Southern Literary Journal* 19 [1] (Fall 1986): 34–45.

10. Mary Tucker to Carr, telephone interview, 12 Oct. 1970.

11. McCullers, "The Flowering Dream: Notes on Writing," in *The Mortgaged Heart* (Boston: Houghton Mifflin, 1971), 281.

12. Whit Burnett to Carr, interview, New York City, 18 Dec. 1970; see also Carr, *The Lonely Hunter: A Biography of Carson McCullers* (New York: Doubleday, 1975), 63.

13. "The Orphanage" was first published in *The Mortgaged Heart*, 49–53.

14. McCullers herself suffered from rheumatic fever—misdiagnosed as tuberculosis—and at fifteen was sent to a sanitarium in Alto, Georgia, to recuperate.

15. Martha Kimbrough Hogan to Carr, interview, Columbus, Ga., 13 October 1970.

16. Lamar Smith to Carr, interview, Perry, Fla., 3 Oct. 1970.

17. McCullers, addendum to "Sucker" and "Court in the West Eighties," in *The Mortgaged Heart*, 29–30.

18. "The Sojourner" was first published in *Mademoiselle* 31 (May 1950): 90, 160–166.

19. Carr, *The Lonely Hunter*, 422–423.

20. Carr, 417–418.

21. Charles and Louise Swick to Carr, interview, Saratoga Springs, N.Y., 21 July 1976.

22. "Art and Mr. Mahoney," was first published in *Mademoiselle* (29 Feb. 1949): 120, 184–186.

23. "A Domestic Dilemma," reprinted in *Collected Stories of Carson McCullers: Including "The Member of the Wedding" and "The Ballad of the Sad Café," 115–127.*

24. Both the town and the cottage described in the story bear a striking resemblance to Nyack, New York, and to McCullers's own house, a house perched above the Hudson at 131 South Broadway in Nyack, in which she lived with Reeves McCullers and her mother.

25. "Who Has Seen the Wind?" was first published in *Mademoiselle* 43 (Sept. 1956): 156–157, 174–188.

26. Before Reeves McCullers killed himself in Paris in 1953, he tried repeatedly to convince his wife to commit suicide with him.

27. "The March," *Redbook* 128 (Mar. 1967): 69, 114–123.

28. The Carson McCullers Collection, Humanities Research Center Library, The University of Texas at Austin.

EPILOGUE

Throughout her adult life, and during much of her childhood, McCullers struggled with what she perceived as man's dual nature: wretched but glorious. She saw man metaphorically as the offspring of a union between Lucifer and God, thus both cursed and blessed. His redemption lay in the way he bore his burden. As McCullers pondered her own blueprint for life and meditated on "origin and choice," she managed to write in 1951—despite an onslaught of new illnesses—a long philosophical poem, "The Dual Angel: A Meditation on Origin and Choice." The poem concludes with a section entitled "Father, Upon Thy Image We Are Spanned":[1]

> Why are we split upon our double nature, how are we
>   planned?
> Father, upon what image are we spanned?
> Turning helpless in the garden of right and wrong
> Mocked by the reversibles of good and evil
> Heir of the exile, Lucifer, and brother of Thy universal Son
> Who said *it is finished* when Thy synthesis was just begun.
> We suffer the sorrow of separation and division
> With a heart that blazes with Christ's vision:
> That though we be deviously natured, dual-planned,
> Father, upon Thy image we are spanned.
>
> AVE

Taken in its entirety, the poem provides both challenge and resolution and serves as a coda to McCullers's life and work. The poem reflects, too, the lyricism found throughout her fiction, a lyricism marked by the dissonant chords organic to her life.

Notes

1. "The Dual Angel: A Meditation on Origin and Choice," *Botteghe Oscure* 9 (1952): 213–218. The poem also appeared in *Mademoiselle* 35 (July 1952): 54–55 and was reprinted in *The Mortgaged Heart,* 288–292. In December 1951, McCullers sent the poem as a Christmas present to her closest friends. This poem reflects, too, her reconciliation with Mary Tucker after fifteen years of estrangement.

BIBLIOGRAPHY

Works by Carson McCullers

Novels and Collections

The Heart Is a Lonely Hunter. Boston: Houghton Mifflin, 1940; London: Cresset, 1943. Novel.

Reflections in a Golden Eye. Boston: Houghton Mifflin, 1941; London: Cresset, 1942. Novel.

The Member of the Wedding. Boston: Houghton Mifflin, 1946; London: Cresset, 1947. Novel.

The Member of the Wedding. New York: New Directions, 1951. Play.

"The Ballad of the Sad Café": The Novels and Stories of Carson McCullers. Boston: Houghton Mifflin, 1951. Includes *The Ballad of the Sad Café* (novella), "Wunderkind," "The Jockey," "Madame Zilensky and the King of Finland," "The Sojourner," "A Domestic Dilemma" (first publication), "A Tree. A Rock. A Cloud," *The Heart Is a Lonely Hunter, Reflections in a Golden Eye, The Member of the Wedding.* Reprinted as *The Shorter Novels and Stories of Carson McCullers.* London: Cresset, 1952; *The Heart Is a Lonely Hunter* omitted. *"The Ballad of the Sad Café" and Collected Short Stories.* Boston: Houghton Mifflin, 1952. The novels are excluded.

The Square Root of Wonderful. Boston: Houghton Mifflin, 1958; London: Cresset, 1958. Play.

Collected Short Stories and the Novel "The Ballad of the Sad Café." Boston: Houghton Mifflin, 1961. Includes "The Haunted Boy," "Wunderkind," "The Jockey," "Madame Zilensky and the King of Finland," "The Sojourner," "A Domestic

Dilemma," "A Tree. A Rock. A Cloud," "The Ballad of the Sad Café" (later retitled *"The Ballad of the Sad Café" and Collected Short Stories*).

Clock Without Hands. Boston: Houghton Mifflin, 1961; London: Cresset, 1961. Novel.

Sweet as a Pickle and Clean as a Pig. Illustrated by Rolf Gerard. Boston: Houghton Mifflin, 1964; London: Cape, 1965. Children's verse.

The Mortgaged Heart, ed. with introduction by Margarita G. Smith. Boston: Houghton Mifflin, 1971; London: Barrie & Jenkins, 1972. Posthumous collection of short fiction ("Sucker," "Court in the West Eighties," "Poldi," "Breath from the Sky," "The Orphanage," "Instant of the Hour After," "Like That," "Wunderkind," "The Aliens," "Untitled Piece," "Author's Outline of 'The Mute,' " "Correspondence," "Art and Mr. Mahoney," "The Haunted Boy," "Who Has Seen the Wind?"); nonfiction ("Look Homeward, Americans," "Night Watch Over Freedom," "Brooklyn Is My Neighborhood," "We Carried Our Banners—We Were Pacifists, Too," "Our Heads Are Bowed," "Home For Christmas," "The Discovery of Christmas," "A Hospital Christmas Eve," "How I Began to Write," "The Russian Realists and Southern Literature," "Loneliness . . . an American Malady," "The Vision Shared," "Isak Dinesen: *Winter's Tales*" (book review), "Isak Dinesen: In Praise of Radiance," "The Flowering Dream: Notes on Writing"; and poetry ("The Mortgaged Heart," "When We Are Lost," "The Dual Angel: A Meditation on Origin and Choice" [a long philosophical poem divided into five short poems: "Incantation to Lucifer," "Hymen, O Hymen," "Love and the Rind of Time," "The Dual Angel," "Father, Upon Thy Image We Are Spanned"], "Stone Is Not Stone"

[a slightly revised version of "The Twisted Trinity," *Decision* 2 (Nov.–Dec. 1941): 30], and "Saraband").
Collected Stories of Carson McCullers: Including "The Member of the Wedding" and "The Ballad of the Sad Café," with introduction by Virginia Spencer Carr. Boston: Houghton Mifflin, 1987. This collection includes every short story published previously except "The March"(published in *Redbook* 128 [Mar. 1967]: 69, 114–123 and reprinted in *Redbook* 137 [Oct. 1971]: 92, 228, 230, 233).

Recordings

"Carson McCullers Reads from *The Member of the Wedding* and Other Works," ed. Jean Stein vanden Heuvel. 1958. M-G-M (E3619 ARC).

Articles (uncollected)

"Books I Remember." *Harper's Bazaar* 75 (Apr. 1941): 82, 122, 125.
"Love's Not Time's Fool" (signed by "A War Wife"). *Mademoiselle* 16 (Apr. 1943): 95, 166–168.
"Author's Note." *New York Times Book Review* (11 June 1961): 4. Discusses *Clock Without Hands.*

Secondary Sources

Selected Works about Carson McCullers

Bibliographies and Checklists

Carr, Virginia Spencer. "Carson McCullers." In *Fifty Southern Writers After 1900: A Bio-Bibliographical Sourcebook,* ed. Robert Bain and Joseph M. Flora, 301–312. Westport, Ct.: Greenwood, 1986. Primary and secondary.
———. "Carson McCullers." In *Contemporary Authors: Bibliographical Series, American Novelists,* Vol. 1, ed. James J. Mar-

tine, 293–345. Detroit: Bruccoli Clark/Gale Research, 1986. Primary and secondary.

———, and Joseph R. Millichap. "Carson McCullers." In *American Women Writers: Fifteen Bibliographical Essays*, ed. Maurice Duke, Jackson R. Bryer, and M. Thomas Inge, 297–319. Westport, Ct.: Greenwood, 1981. Primary and secondary.

Shapiro, Adrian M., Jackson R. Bryer, and Kathleen Field. *Carson McCullers: A Descriptive Listing and Annotated Bibliography of Criticism*. New York: Garland, 1980. Primary and secondary.

Selected Interviews

Balakian, Nona. "Carson McCullers Completes New Novel Despite Adversity." *New York Times*, 3 Sept. 1961, 46.

Breit, Harvey. "Behind the Wedding—Carson McCullers Discusses the Novel She Converted into a Stage Play." *New York Times*, 1 Jan. 1950, sec. 2, p. 3.

"*The Marquis* Interviews Carson McCullers." *Marquis* (Lafayette College), 1964, 5–6, 20–23.

Reed, Rex. " 'Frankie Addams' at 50." *New York Times*, 16 Apr. 1967, sec. 2, p. 15.

White, Terence de Vere. "With Carson McCullers: Terence de Vere White Interviews the American Novelist at the Home of Her Host, John Huston." *Irish Times* (Dublin), 10 Apr. 1967, 12.

Biographies

Carr, Virginia Spencer. *The Lonely Hunter: A Biography of Carson McCullers*. Garden City: Doubleday, 1975; London: Peter Owen, 1976; New York: Carroll & Graf, 1985. A thorough and carefully researched biography; the most comprehensive book on McCullers to date.

Evans, Oliver. *Carson McCullers: Her Life and Work*. London:

Peter Owen, 1965. Republished as *The Ballad of Carson McCullers.* New York: Coward-McCann, 1966. First book-length study; analyzes each book in detail, discusses many of the short stories, and summarizes the most notable critical responses.

Books on McCullers

Cook, Richard. *Carson McCullers.* New York: Ungar, 1975. Excellent introduction to McCullers, which includes the life, plot summaries, analytical discussions of each major work, and an objective overview of career.

Edmonds, Dale. *Carson McCullers.* Austin: Steck-Vaughn, 1969. Reliable biographical essay and plot summaries of major works and judicious interpretations; insists that McCullers not be treated as a regionalist.

Graver, Lawrence. *Carson McCullers.* Minneapolis: University of Minnesota Press, 1969. A reliable introduction to McCullers's life and works.

McDowell, Margaret B. *Carson McCullers.* New York: Twayne, 1980. The best critical overview of McCullers's work to date; provides excellent general introduction to the writer and a scholarly analysis of each major work; significant feminist perspective.

Westling, Louise. *Sacred Groves and Ravaged Gardens: The Fiction of Eudora Welty, Carson McCullers, and Flannery O'Conner.* Athens: University of Georgia Press, 1985. Convincingly extends her argument regarding McCullers's "rebellious tomboys" and other androgynous characters and is one of the best feminist literary studies published to date.

Wikborg, Eleanor. *"The Member of the Wedding": Aspects of Structure and Style.* Gothenburg Studies in English, 31. Goteborg, Sweden: Acta, Univeritatus Gothoburgensis, 1975; Atlantic Highlands, N.J.: Humanities Press, 1975. Isolates the significant structural and stylistic features of *The Member of the Wedding* and examines the explicit and implicit development of symbols and their interaction on the literal and symbolic levels of meaning; illustrates the potential for other linguistic studies of McCullers's work.

Selected Articles and Book Sections on McCullers

Baldanza, Frank. "Plato in Dixie." *Georgia Review* 12 (Summer 1958): 151–167. Sees elements of Plato's *Symposium* and *Phaedrus* in each major work; notes parallels between author's "science of love" in "A Tree. A Rock. A Cloud" and Plato's dialogues.

Buchen, Irving H. "Divine Collusion: The Art of Carson McCullers." *Dalhousie Review* 54 (Autumn 1974): 529–541. Examines McCullers's essay "The Flowering Dream: Notes on Writing" for her aesthetics; finds her artistic theory so entangled in the religious quest that he must view aesthetics and metaphysics at the same time.

Carr, Virginia Spencer. "Carson McCullers and *The Heart Is a Lonely Hunter*: An Introduction." Pamphlet introduction to Southern Classics Library Edition of *The Heart Is a Lonely Hunter.* Birmingham: Oxmoor, 1984.

———. "Carson McCullers: Novelist Turned Playwright." *South Atlantic Quarterly* 46 (Fall 1987): 22–31.

Dedmond, Francis B. "Doing Her Own Thing: Carson McCullers' Dramatization of 'The Member of the Wedding.' " *South Atlantic Bulletin* 40 (May 1975): 47–52. Compares judiciously the significant differences between the novel and the play.

Dodd, Wayne D. "The Development of Theme Through Symbol in the Novels of Carson McCullers." *Georgia Review* 17 (Summer 1963): 206–213. Responds to Frank Durham's essay regarding Singer's role as God in *The Heart Is a Lonely*

Hunter; suggests that in McCullers's depiction of an endless progression of gods there is a "pseudo-metaphysical basis" for the "total lack of understanding and communication between man and man."

Drake, Robert. "The Lonely Heart of Carson McCullers." *Christian Century* 85 (10 Jan. 1968): 50–51. Views McCullers's weakness as an inability to impose form consistently upon her "one theme of spiritual isolation."

Durham, Frank. "God and No God in *The Heart Is a Lonely Hunter*." *South Atlantic Quarterly* 56 (Autumn 1957): 494–499. Treats novel as an "ironic religious allegory"; sees both mutes as Gods who neither understand their suppliants nor communicate with them.

Emerson, Donald. "The Ambiguities of *Clock Without Hands*." *Wisconsin Studies in Contemporary Literature* 3 (Fall 1962): 15–28. Addresses McCullers's strengths in dealing with the inward experience and her comprehension of the human, rather than the social, condition.

Evans, Oliver. "The Achievement of Carson McCullers." *English Journal* 51 (May 1962): 302–308. Extends his earlier argument regarding author's literary contribution to help counter negative criticism of *Clock Without Hands*; says McCullers writes so realistically that readers miss the point that she must, ultimately, be taken as an allegorical writer.

Fletcher, Mary Dell. "Carson McCullers' 'Ancient Mariner.' " *South Central Bulletin* 35 (Winter 1975): 123–125. Treats "A Tree. A Rock. A Cloud" as a modern version of Coleridge's "Ancient Mariner."

Folk, Barbara Nauer. "The Sad Sweet Music of Carson McCullers." *Georgia Review* 16 (Summer 1962): 202–209. Finds McCullers's use of music and musical references and allusions her symbol of the ideal.

Hassan, Ihab. "Carson McCullers: The Alchemy of Love and Aesthetics of Pain." *Modern Fiction Studies* 5 (Winter 1959–1960): 311–325. Reprinted in revised form in his *Radical Innocence: Studies in the Contemporary American Novel.* Princeton: Princeton University Press, 1961: pp. 205–229. A significant essay that treats McCullers's use of the Gothic as "spiritual or transcendental" and explores the retreat of her lonely characters into their "inner rooms," a denial of Eros and thus an intensification of the pain.

MacDonald, Edgar E. "The Symbolic Unity of *The Heart Is a Lonely Hunter,*" in *A Festschrift for Professor Marguerite Roberts, on the Occasion of Her Retirement from Westhampton College, University of Richmond, Virginia,* ed. Frieda Elaine Penninger. Richmond: University of Richmond, 1976. 168–187. Examines the generalizations of recent criticism and concludes that no one has looked carefully at the hagiography or analyzed the structure in terms of the implied sainthood of its characters other than John Singer; provides a careful Gnostic reading of the novel.

McPherson, Hugo. "Carson McCullers: Lonely Huntress." *Tamarack Review* 11 (Spring 1959): 28–40. Treats the inherent incompatibility of the spiritual and physical aspects of McCullers's lonely seekers whose anguish is intensified by their ambiguous sexual identities.

Madden, David. "The Paradox of the Need for privacy and the Need for Understanding in Carson McCullers' *The Heart Is a Lonely Hunter.*" *Literature and Psychology* 17, nos. 2–3. (1967): 128–140. Traces the subtle patterns of attraction and repulsion among the characters and explores the paradox of their insatiable need for human understanding, yet also for an "inviolable privacy."

Millichap, Joseph R. "The Realistic Structure of *The Heart Is a*

Lonely Hunter." *Twentieth Century Literature* 17 (Jan. 1971): 11–17. A careful analysis of the novel's structure that reveals how all elements of the character, plot, style, setting, and symbol are integrated to present the "failure of communication, the isolation, and the violence prevalent in modern society."

Moore, Jack B. "Carson McCullers: The Heart Is a Timeless Hunter." *Twentieth Century Literature* 11 (July 1965): 76–81. Emphasizes the successful use of the myth of initiation in contemporary terms and likens Mick's journey to the romances and initiation tales of Hawthorne and Poe.

Paden, Frances Freeman. "Autistic Gestures in *The Heart Is a Lonely Hunter.*" *Modern Fiction Studies* 28 (Autumn 1982): 453–463. Notes that all of the major characters exhibit autistic gestures and direct their frustrations and bodily gestures increasingly upon themselves; distinguishes between a character's unconscious self-mutilation and his deliberate self-inflicted wounds.

Phillips, Robert. "Freaking Out: The Short Stories of Carson McCullers." *Southwest Review* 63 (Winter 1978): 65–73. Discusses McCullers's nineteen published stories in which her characters appear normal to the eye, but are "symbolically grotesque"; both adults and youths alike "freak out" and become hardened rebels when they realize that they are destined ever to be "outsiders."

Presley, Delma Eugene. "Carson McCullers' Descent to the Earth." *Descant* 17 (Fall 1972): 54–60. Defends *Clock Without Hands* against what critics called McCullers's "effete skepticism"; contends that she abandoned her skepticism for affirmation and a belief in reconciliatory power, but was unable to find a suitable artistic technique.

Roberts, Mary. "Imperfect Androgyny and Imperfect Love in the Works of Carson McCullers." *University of Hartford*

Studies in Literature 12 (1980): 73–98. Contends that McCullers portrays neither the true androgyne nor the hermaphrodite, but an "incomplete androgyne" unhappily incarcerated with a dualistic nature that he tries desperately to break free of by "imagining a beloved who can make him or her whole."

Rubin, Louis D., Jr. "Carson McCullers: The Aesthetic of Pain." *Virginia Quarterly Review* 53 (Spring 1977): 265–283. Reprinted in his *A Gallery of Southerners*. Baton Rouge: Louisiana State University Press, 1982: pp. 135–151. One of the most judicious and compelling essays on McCullers since her death. Assesses McCullers's art—book by book—and why it eventually broke down, the key lying in how McCullers herself perceived pain.

Smith, C. Michael. " 'A Voice in a Fugue': Characters and Musical Structure in Carson McCullers' *The Heart Is a Lonely Hunter*." *Modern Fiction Studies* 25 (Summer 1979): 258–263. Likens the novel's careful structure to the polyphonic pattern of a fugue (as McCullers herself did in her outline to "The Mute") and demonstrates how it works throughout.

Taylor, Horace. "*The Heart Is a Lonely Hunter*: A Southern Waste Land." *Studies in American Literature* 8 (1960): 154–60; 172–73. Addresses each character's deeply rooted narcissism and their making of Singer a "homemade god."

Vickery, John B. "Carson McCullers: A Map of Love." *Wisconsin Studies in Contemporary Literature* 1 (Winter 1960): 13–24. Treats McCullers's canon in terms of her "total vision of love" and distinguishes each novel's vision from the other.

Walker, Sue B. "The Link in the Chain Called Love: A New Look at Carson McCullers' Novels." *Mark Twain Journal* 18 (Winter 1976): 8–12. Uses "A Tree. A Rock. A Cloud" as basis for a convincing discussion of McCullers's central metaphor, a chain constructed with "links of love," and draws from each major work except *Reflections in a Golden Eye* to support her thesis of love.

Westling, Louise. "Carson McCullers' Tomboys." *Southern Humanities Review* 14 (Fall 1980): 339–350. Examines the crisis of identity by Mick and Frankie, who share artistic temperaments and serious ambitions as tomboys until "safe conformity triumphs" and they are forced to give up their boyish ways and creativeness.

Williams, Tennessee. "This Book." Introduction to McCullers's *Reflections in a Golden Eye.* New York: New Directions, 1950: pp. vii–xvii: Thinks *The Ballad of the Sad Café* and *The Member of the Wedding* are better books, but commends *Reflections in a Golden Eye* for its mastery over a "youthful lyricism" and defends McCullers against accusations of morbidity.

Young, Marguerite. "Metaphysical Fiction." *Kenyon Review* 9 (Winter 1947): 151–155. The most significant and convincing early study of McCullers's first four books from which much serious criticism evolved.

INDEX

INDEX

INDEX